Critical
Essays
in
Modern
Literature

TITLES IN THE SERIES

William Faulkner: An Estimate of His Contributions to the Modern American Novel
Mary Cooper Robb

The Fiction of John O'Hara
E. Russell Carson

The Fiction and Criticism of Katherine Anne Porter (Revised)
Harry J. Mooney, Jr.

The Hero in Hemingway's Short Stories
Joseph DeFalco

Entrances to Dylan Thomas' Poetry
Ralph Maud

James Gould Cozzens: Novelist of Intellect
Harry J. Mooney, Jr.

Joyce Cary: The Comedy of Freedom
Charles G. Hoffmann

The Short Stories of Ambrose Bierce
Stuart C. Woodruff

The Fiction of J. D. Salinger (Revised)
Frederick L. Gwynn
and Joseph L. Blotner

The Novels of Anthony Powell
Robert K. Morris

James Agee: Promise and Fulfillment
Kenneth Seib

Richard Wright: An Introduction to the Man and His Works
Russell Carl Brignano

Dylan Thomas' Early Prose: A Study in Creative Mythology
Annis Pratt

DYLAN THOMAS' EARLY PROSE

Dylan Thomas'
Early Prose

A Study in Creative Mythology

ANNIS PRATT

ISBN 0–8229–3198–2 (cloth)
ISBN 0–8229–5215–7 (paper)
Library of Congress Catalog Card Number: 71–101191
Copyright © 1970, University of Pittsburgh Press
Manufactured in the United States of America

Grateful acknowledgment is made for permission to quote material
that appears in:
Dylan Thomas, *Adventures in the Skin Trade*. Copyright 1955
© 1964 by New Directions.
Dylan Thomas, *The Collected Poems*. Copyright 1939, 1943, 1946
by New Directions. Copyright 1952, 1953 by Dylan Thomas.
Dylan Thomas, *The Notebooks*. © 1956, 1966, 1967 by the
Trustees for the Copyrights of Dylan Thomas (© 1966, 1967
by Ralph Maud, for "Introduction" and "Notes").
All reprinted by permission of New Directions Publishing Corpora-
tion.

Quotations in Appendix C are from the periodical *transition*, published in Paris, 1927–1938.

For William York Tindall

Contents

Preface   xi

Introduction: Biography and the Problem of
Influence   3

I: The Structure of the Early Prose   30

II: Mythology in the Early Prose   52

III: Religion in the Early Prose   85

IV: Blake and the Occult in the Early Prose   104

V: Surrealism as a Literary Method   129

VI: The Later Prose and Narrative Poetry   149

APPENDIX A: A Comparative Chronology of the
Prose and Poetry   173

APPENDIX B: The Critics and the Problem of
Influence   184

APPENDIX C: Some Notes on the Contents of
transition, 1929–1936   191

Notes   197

Bibliography   211

Index   221

Preface

Some question may be raised concerning the scope
of this book, in which I limit myself to a consideration of Dylan Thomas' early prose and its effects upon the early and later poetry. Is there not, I have
been asked, a prose "canon" making it exigent that I
devote as much time to the "beloved" later prose as
to the controversial earlier pieces? My position on
the later prose of Dylan Thomas should be understood from the outset—I consider it, like the film
scripts, an inferior side branch of his total work.
Whereas the early prose, finished by 1939, can be
taken as a part of the symbolic universe of both the
early and later poetry, the later prose—under which
I include the *Portrait of the Artist as a Young Dog*,
"Adventures in the Skin Trade" (published in 1941 in
Folios of New Writing and later as the title piece to
a volume of prose mainly of early composition), and

Under Milk Wood—represents a departure into a mode of writing that, had Thomas lived, he might well have developed into a richer branch of his opus. As it stands, however, it represents a number of interesting attempts at what must be taken as a minor genre within his writing. It is not totally unimportant to the consideration of Thomas' achievement, and since in this study I intend to discuss the relevance of the early prose to Thomas' total work, I will devote some space to the later prose in my concluding chapter.

*   *   *

I would like to acknowledge the time and concern which Professors John Unterecker, Robert Gorham Davis, and William York Tindall of Columbia University gave to the dissertation version of this book.

To William York Tindall I dedicate this volume in appreciation of his scholarship and of his aid in obtaining the fellowships, scholarships, and loans without which a study of this kind could not have been undertaken.

The librarians of Wellesley College not only made their full resources available to my research but uncovered valuable material on their own. I am grateful also for the material supplied by Leslie Rees of the Swansea Public Libraries, by Glyn Jones of Whitchurch, Glamorgan, and by Lady Pamela Snow. To David Posner of the Lockwood Memorial Library at the State University of New York at Buffalo and to

William A. Jackson of the Houghton Memorial Library at Harvard University I owe thanks for making their manuscript collections available to me. Professor Donald Tritschler of Skidmore College provided invaluable information concerning Dylan Thomas' Red Notebook. I am grateful further for his close reading and editing, which have been crucial to preparation of the final draft of this book. I am deeply indebted also to Professor Robert Adolph who travelled to Swansea for interviews and research. I would like to thank my Spelman College students for their creativity in studying the relation between Thomas' early prose and his poetry.

I wish to thank New Directions for its permission to quote extensively from *Adventures in the Skin Trade* (1961), the *Collected Poems of Dylan Thomas* (1957), and *The Notebooks of Dylan Thomas* (1967).

Finally, I wish to acknowledge with deepest gratitude the faithful correspondence and continued enthusiasm of Professor Ralph N. Maud of Simon Fraser University, Burnaby, British Columbia, whose advice and scholarship allowed me to penetrate far deeper into the mysteries of Dylan Thomas' work than otherwise would have been possible.

DYLAN THOMAS' EARLY PROSE

"Creative mythology . . . springs not, like theology, from the dicta of authority, but from the insights, sentiments, thought, and vision of an adequate individual, loyal to his own experience of value. Thus it corrects the authority holding to the shells of forms produced and left behind by lives once lived. Renewing the act of experience itself, it restores to existence the quality of adventure, at once shattering and reintegrating the fixed, already known, in the sacrificial creative fire of the becoming thing that is no thing at all but life, not as it will be or as it should be, as it was or as it never will be, but as it is, in depth, in process, here and now, inside and out."

Joseph Campbell, Creative Mythology

Biography and
the Problem of Influence

"We can eliminate biography as a relevant fact about poetic organization only if we consider the work of art as if it were written neither by people nor for people, involving neither inducements nor resistances. Such can be done, but the cost is tremendous in so far as the critic considers it his task to disclose the poem's eventfulness."

Kenneth Burke, The Philosophy of Literary Form

I

Dylan Thomas is most often remembered as a Falstaffian, bar-hopping hail-fellow-well-met, an impression which he did his best to encourage in his conversations and autobiographical statements. A considerable number of the memoirs published shortly after his death stress his irrepressible gaiety and social impishness, as if he had been a Peter Pan whom no one had thought able to die.[1] The death that shocked Thomas' admirers would not have surprised the poet, who had early faced the "worm beneath my nail" and incorporated it into a vision which was akin to the tragic gaiety of Yeats. No one is his own best biographer, and if, as in Thomas' case, he is given to weaving myths about himself, his friends become an equally doubtful source of evidence. As Aneiran Talfan Davies pointed out in a refreshingly candid if prophetic note, "Dylan Thomas was a leg-

3

end *before* he died, and the biographers and academic researchers of the future are going to have a whale of a time sorting things out."[2]

Constantine FitzGibbon's "official biography" appeared in 1965. (The family allowed him the sole access to most of the crucial material which they hold.) It provides a picture of Thomas' life as a psychological totality from the early childhood days to the agon in New York City. FitzGibbon does not intend the biography as a work of criticism, however, and makes little critical connection between the events of Thomas' life and the symbolic, inner world of his poetry and prose. I would hope that someone will step forward to do for Thomas' life and work what Richard Ellmann has so brilliantly done for Yeats and Joyce; for the moment we are left, as in the first decade after Thomas' death, with the spectacle of the formally educated critic doing a mystery dance around the works of the informally educated poet, a spectacle which would have amused the poet. We are, moreover, still badly in need of facts concerning Thomas' early reading (see pp. 10–13) and whatever other sources might have provided the raw material for his personal symbolic universe.

"He had the big advantage too over displaced Artists," writes Caitlin Thomas, ". . . that he worked in a fanatically narrow groove, . . . the groove of direct hereditary descent in the land of his birth, which he never in thought, and hardly in body, moved out of. Which handed him his line of approach ready made, and his poems already matured inside him."[3] Although a thorough essay in biographical criticism is beyond the scope of this study, the early prose is infused with all of the events and influences of Thomas' early life in Wales. In spite of the general acceptance of the fact that Thomas did not speak or read the Welsh language, it seems appropriate to begin with a consideration of the Welsh environment in which he spent his early years.

Dylan Thomas lived in a region that was rich not only in folklore but in the origins of folklore; as a boy he explored a landscape shaped by prehistoric floods and marked by sites of prehistoric, druid, sabbatic, and Christian legend. During his father's boyhood the skeleton of a "red lady" had been found surrounded by mammoth tusks in the glacial age caves beneath Gower Peninsula, near Swansea. The hummock of Cefn Y Bryn with its "druid well" and reputed "King Arthur's stone" also rises out of the Gower Peninsula, while the countryside of Glamorgan and Carmarthenshire, where many of his relatives lived, is full of landmarks reputedly built by the druids.

Dylan Thomas' paternal grandfather, Evan Thomas, was a railway guard at Johnstown, a suburb of Carmarthen.[4] This city had served for a long time as cultural and administrative center for the west of Wales; it was a Roman and Norman stronghold and, before that, the ecclesiastical center of the druid religion. Merlin reputedly presided there as archdruid, and the *Black Book of Carmarthen* (which Thomas parodies in "The Orchards" as "The Black Book of Llaregubb") was discovered in its priory of Black Canons. The contents of this and other

books of folklore had been expounded at the beginning of the nineteenth century by Edward Davies
in *The Mythology and Rites of the British Druids*
and *Celtic Researches on the Origin, Traditions and
Language of the Ancient Britons*. It has been con-
jectured that Dylan Thomas might have read these
two volumes along with Williams ab Ithel's translation of *Y Barddas*;[5] *Celtic Researches* contains a
number of Thomases from the Johnstown area in its
original list of subscribers (for what, in Wales, that
is worth). Although there is no evidence whatsoever that Thomas actually read these works,[6] the
abundance of analogies between his symbolic universe and that romanticized by the nineteenth-
century "researchers" has led me to devote Chapters
2 and 3 of this study to the possible influence of
Welsh folklore and pre-Christian druid religion upon
his early prose and poetry.

Cults of the "horned god," if we accept Miss
Margaret Murray's account, continued to exist in
Wales alongside of the comparatively austere "bardo-
druidic" tradition.[7] "At least one coven of nine wild
women seems to have been active in South Wales
during early medieval times," writes Robert Graves,[8]
and in the 1960's the appearance of Sybil Leek and
her Sherwood Forest Covens suggests that witchery
in Great Britain has never been dead, merely dormant. In his earliest poems Thomas is in terror of
the witches, vampires, devils, and damned who
formed part of the folk tradition of South Wales.
These supernatural figures play an important part in
the stories which I shall consider in Chapter 4.

The strongest religious influence in the Carmarthen area and in Swansea was the Christianity of the Protestant chapels, most of which had been founded during the Methodist revival of the eighteenth century. Mr. and Mrs. Evan Thomas, who attended the Heol Awst Congregational Chapel, were probably as rigorous chapel people as most at that time. In 1904 a revival was set off near Carmarthen and spread to fill the whole of Wales with field preachers and writhing converts (a spectacle not unfamiliar to the American South and West). The souls who would not repent were attacked by larger and larger phalanxes of those who had recently confronted their Maker, and the accounts in the *Western Mail* treat with particular relish the fiery confessions of atheists and agnostics who were finally brought to their knees.[9]

The great number of professed nonbelievers in Wales in the early twentieth century was due not only to the lax years that preceded the revival but also to a wholly modern phenomenon, the "new learning." In the late nineteenth century the works of Spencer, Darwin, and Huxley had been translated into Welsh, and at the same time that the 1904 revival was raging the liberal agnostics had quietly taken over the Welsh educational system from university to grammar school.[10] With the new learning came a new pantheistic theology, preached by R. J. Campbell, who insisted upon the "Immanence of God instead of the Transcendency of God —i.e., that God was not a person, standing outside the creation and looking down from heaven upon man, but was, in fact, in the universe and part of it, to be found in all things animate and inanimate."[11] Reverence for the innate goodness of nature was not new to Wales and Ireland. As Joseph Campbell reminds us, and as we shall explore further in Chapter 3, the bards and druids had combined Christianity with their own more stoic theology, retaining a conviction of the divinity in man and nature that gave rise to the Pelagian heresy.[12]

The liberal movement in theology impressed both Thomas' great-uncle and his father, who probably accomplished the first rebellions in the family from traditional piety. Great-Uncle William Thomas, Evan Thomas' brother, became a Unitarian minister. "Liberal in theology" and "radical in politics," he was also a schoolmaster and poet, thus combining the theology, politics, and vocations of his nephew, David John, and his great-nephew, Dylan. He gave himself the bardic pen name of Gwilym Marles, the surname being the name of a stream near his birthplace in the west of Wales.[13] Thomas did not tell any stories about this remarkable relative, perhaps because he wanted to be thought of as the first rebel-poet in his family. Instead, he told everyone that Grandfather Evan was a preacher, thus inventing a mythical combination of grandfather and great-uncle, who as Aneiran Davies rightly prophesied "is going to stomp around quite a lot of future writings on the poet." Great-Uncle Gwilym Marles was transformed into Marlais of "The Orchards" and perhaps also into the promiscuous great-uncle, Jarvis, whose home, like Great-Uncle William's, was in the country fields of Wales, and who is the progenitor of several of Dylan Thomas' prose heroes.

Whereas William Thomas was a Unitarian preacher, David John Thomas, his nephew, became an atheist. He left Johnstown for the University of Wales, where he received an honors degree in English literature. He devoted his life to the grammar school system, taking up his first position as English master at Swansea in 1899 and remaining there, except for a year at Pontypridd, until his retirement in 1936. He was an instructor of rigorous standards, beloved for his scholarly enthusiasm if not for his irascibility. His son Dylan, who decided early to be a poet, shared his love for literature, if not for things academic.

Although it has been assumed—undoubtedly at his own suggestion—that Dylan Thomas "fell" straight from the chapel to the pub, it seems likely that his upbringing was considerably complicated by his father's earlier transition from country to city and from piety to atheism. At some time in his early boyhood Dylan may have willingly participated in chapel and Sunday school (he describes a Sunday school certificate which he was later ashamed to have hanging on his wall). Certainly his absorption of biblical material suggests more than token piety. His mother was devout, and he was thus brought up in the same type of family tension as William Butler Yeats, whose mother tried to offset his father's freethinking. He may also have experienced the conversion of personal confrontation with Christ so common to Welsh Methodism, for two of his finest poems, "Vision and Prayer" and "In country sleep," are written from a passionate conviction of the existence of a saviour in whom he does not want to believe. Personal confrontation with the diety might have engendered Thomas' always personal approach to Christ, but if indeed he experienced a religious crisis, it was soon mingled with the other strands of a unique theology which I will discuss in Chapter 3.

Thomas' London acquaintances tend to be scornful of the idea that he read anything but detective stories, thrillers, and his own poetry at any time.[14] Daniel Jones, on the other hand, mentions W. H. Davies, Yeats, Aldington, Sacheverell Sitwell, Lawrence, Hopkins, and many others as poets whose works he read and imitated.[15] From the evidence of the early Poetry Notebooks I would add the imagists, Auden, and Blake. The *Selected Letters of Dylan Thomas*, edited by Constantine FitzGibbon, reveals a young man so well read that literary references merge naturally with the other topics of his correspondence. "My education was the liberty I had to read indiscriminately and all the time," wrote Thomas, whose readings must have included the library of his father's "brown study," where they took place; "I never could have dreamed that there were such goings-on, such do's and argiebargies, such love and sense and terror and humbug, such and so many blinding bright lights breaking across the just awaking wits."[16] What might have been the contents of David John Thomas' library? The final examinations at Swansea Grammar School involved an optional selection of "Welsh Literature and History," the reading list including a number of books on the folklore of Wales, in Welsh. Two interesting titles on the list are William Rowland's *Chwedau Gwerin Cymru* [Folk stories of Wales] and Arglwydd Rhys' *Yns Yr Hud u Chaneuon Eraill* [The island of delight and other stories]. One might hazard a guess that Thomas senior, who was given to reading Shakespeare by his son's sickbed, might have translated at least the titles for his son, whose poetry and prose exhibit a continuing fascination with mysterious island landscapes. It seems doubtful, since everyone agrees that Dylan Thomas had no Welsh whatsoever, that he could have perused them for himself.

It seems likely that sometime before the age of fifteen Thomas immersed himself in the tales of Machen,[17] de la Mare, and whatever writers he could find who dealt with the legends of Egypt and Wales. Oscar Williams tells us that Thomas knew *The Book of the Dead*,[18] and besides the *Mabinogion*[19] he may have read some such compendium of tales for the young as Baikie's *Wonder Tales of the Ancient World*. The style of both the early and later prose seems to owe something to the tales of Caradoc Evans and T. F. Powys, two Welsh writers whose principal works were published before or during Thomas' adolescence[20] (see pp. 45–48). It is my impression that after about his sixteenth year Thomas' period of heavy readings in legend and English literature, which he drew upon for the rest of his life, was over.

The supernatural "thrillers" of Machen, with their peculiar combination of Huysmans, Pater, *The Quest del Saint Graal*, and Sherlock Holmes, seem to have been an important influence on Thomas' early prose. Born in Caerlon-on-Usk, Machen divided his life between pursuit of a literary career in London and periodic returns to the border of Wales which remained the source of his inspiration. From his childhood Machen was fond of imagining ancient rituals that might have taken place in the Roman ruins and prehistoric "circles" near his home. Most of his stories take a detached and civilized narrator away from London to discover some weird rite still enacted in the Welsh countryside. Although occasionally, as in *The Secret Glory*, the quest is for the high rites of the Holy Grail, usually Machen's heroes are faced with the horror of a sabbatic sacrifice.

Machen's *Hill of Dreams*, an autobiographical novel about writing a novel, resembles Thomas' "The Orchards" so closely that it may have inspired that complex tale which was central to the early prose.[21] The hero Lucian struggles, like Thomas' Marlais, to get his dream of a Welsh Byzantium down on paper; like several of Thomas' prose heroes, he is enchanted by a country girl who initiates him into the rites of love; and this creature, capable of infinite feminine tenderness and yet sister to the hag of destruction, becomes a Queen of the Sabbath quite similar to the figure who dominates nearly every one of Thomas' early tales. Machen's prose descriptions of Lucian's dream world flow like chants of some forgotten litany; in much the same way, Thomas' tales, centering upon ritual actions, are written in a prose-verse that flows in careful strophes towards a sacramental climax.

In an autobiographical note Machen states that his literary efforts arose from an attempt to "invent a story which would recreate those vague impressions of wonder and awe and mystery that I myself had received from the form and shape of the land in boyhood and youth."[22] Thomas' early tales are highly dependent upon a landscape whose "form and shape" is both anatomical and mythological. As we shall see, its valleys, hills, streams, and periodic floods are analogous to the events of the female body, extended as a metaphorical landscape over which the heroes quest as "folkmen" for both sexual fulfillment and poetic inspiration. The narratives are not governed wholly by personal sexual motivation, but like Machen's tales they bristle with details apparently adapted from mythological, theological, or occult tradition.

In later poems such as "Fern Hill" Thomas suggests a "green and carefree" childhood, but only near the end of his life was he able to idealize youth a bit and to laugh at the agonies of the adolescent. Even then his recollected exuberance was considerably qualified by memories of restrictions, fears, and shocks to innocence. The young boy of "The Peaches," "A Visit to Granpa's," "Patricia, Edith, and Arnold" and "The Fight" (all published during 1938 and 1939; see Appendix A) is already a witness to infidelity, drunkenness, and madness. He may run about the fields carefree in the daytime, but at night he tries to exorcize the demons that burn in his head by putting them into stories.

In 1930 Thomas began the first of four manuscript copybooks, writing out by hand the poems which, often enough, he did not choose to publish in the school newspaper. There are four of these poetry copybooks—now available in Ralph Maud's work, *The Notebooks of Dylan Thomas*—the 1930 Notebook, 1930–1932 Notebook, February 1933 Notebook, and August 1933 Notebook. From Dr. Maud's description of these copybooks and from Dr. Donald Tritschler's study of the Red Notebook of prose, we are able to realize for the first time the importance of their contents to the critical understanding of Thomas' early development.[23]

Until he was fifteen Thomas' experience was probably as limited as that of any boy who watches love and hate, death and sensuality through other people's windows. The events that underly the earliest Notebooks, however, shattered his boyish remove and turned him, by the age of sixteen, into a bitterly disillusioned young man. Many of the entries in the first Notebook (April–December 1930) are characterized by an imitative fragility; the gentle sensualism of Swinburne presides over Thomas' first conquests, and there are even occasional pieces about shepherds and shepherdesses. From such entries as "Poem Written on the Death of a Very Dear Illusion" (May 1930), however, it is clear that he was becoming disenchanted. Disgust and horror swiftly replaced the ladylove, gazelles, and litanies of boyish sexual idealism, while

Machen's demons and sabbath sorceresses replaced the bucolics. With the first entry in the second Notebook (December 1930 to April 1932) he had begun to feel that he had given over his poetic power along with his innocence to the clutches of a savage sensuality. There are references to sodomy and homosexuality and a note of the sadism that would later find its way into "The Vest" and "The True Story."

The Pre-Raphaelite delicacy with which Thomas had treated intercourse in the first Notebook was replaced in the second by disgusted anguish at the conception of cancerous embryos. By the summer of 1931 he had recoiled from the vampires and Liliths entangling him, and in the last entry (April 1932) the devil himself had broken everything left whole, leaving the young poet's imagination cluttered with the cigarette butts and broken bottles of adolescent debauch.

With the poems of the summer of 1931 Thomas began to achieve an intensity of line and abstraction of imagery that is quite different from the discursive, prosaic style of earlier entries. Sharp images of embittered sensuality are knit together in the antithetical clusters that characterize the later writing. Here, however, there is a quality of trance about the way the elements are thrown together, as if directly from an anguished mind in which rational connections have been unsettled. Whether or not these poems reflect biographical events or fantasies of adolescence, it is evident that Dylan Thomas was victim of an unusually profound shock to his innocent assumptions about life. I am reminded of the scatalogical diatribes written by the young Rimbaud after suffering an "undefined moral shock" during his first trip to Paris in 1871.[24] The affinity between the biography and works of the two poets perhaps springs from their common experience of an unusually sensitive adolescence.

"It might be argued," suggests Derek Stanford, "that the real flowering of the poet's dionysian *alter-ego* took place after what Sir Max Beerbohm describes as 'the great apocalyptic moment of initiation into the fabulous metropolis.' "[25] Certainly Thomas' short story about London, "Prologue to an Adventure" (1937), is apocalyptic in conception. His first visit may have been for a few weeks in August 1933, although it is not impossible that he might have gone up to London briefly in 1931. His first longer stay was from February 23 to March 5, 1934, and by 1935 he was making frequent trips back and forth between city and country.[26]

As early as 1934, one acquaintance assures us, Thomas turned to the "extreme avant-garde, to Joyce and the Paris magazine *transition*."[27] Mr. Keidrych Rhys tells us that Dylan Thomas "was always fascinated by its [*transition*'s] published work in back issues which he borrowed."[28] A perusal of these back issues from 1927 to 1938 provides a wealth of literary history (see Appendix C). Such authors as André Breton, James Joyce, Samuel Beckett, and Franz Kafka contributed regularly, as well as such lesser figures as William Saroyan, Jacques Barzun, and Kay Boyle. A great deal of attention was paid to psychology and art—Carl Jung as well as Hans Arp and Wassily Kandinsky wrote for its pages. An "Inquiry into the Spirit and Language of the Night" included in the spring 1938 issue (no. 27) was answered, among other writers, by Sherwood Anderson, Kenneth Burke, Malcolm Cowley, T. S. Eliot, Michael Gold, Ernest Hemingway, Robinson Jeffers, and Archibald MacLeish.

It was thus into a literary London temporarily steeped in surrealism that Dylan Thomas plunged during his earliest visits—a London of psychedelic parties that would not be unfamiliar to the inhabitants of Haight-Asbury and the East Village of the sixties. On December 9, 1935, nonetheless, he wrote in response to Richard Church's letter concerning the surrealist elements in his poetry that "I am not, never have been, never will be, or could be for that matter, a surrealist. . . . I have very little idea what surrealism is; until quite recently I had never heard of it; I have never, to my knowledge, read even a paragraph of surrealist literature."[29] By 1936, however, he had attended the surrealist exhibition with Vernon Watkins (where Thomas offered around tea brewed of string) and was invited to give a reading with Eluard and others at a surrealist poetry gathering in July of the same year.[30] It was at this same time that he was preparing "The Mouse and the Woman" for publication in the fall issue of *transition*.

By 1938, moreover, he was praising Henry Treece for his chapter devoted to surrealism in *Dylan Thomas: "Dog Among the Fairies"*: "I think the method you adopted in the surrealist chapter—the clearing away of superficial misconceptions by attack and contrast of quotations—is the only effective one . . . ,"[31] suggesting that he now understood, at least, the nature of his affinities to, and his differences from, the surrealist movement. As we shall see in Chapter 5 he was later to arrive at a fully developed critical position on surrealism as a literary method.

We know from his "Answers to an Enquiry" that appeared in the October 1934 issue of *New Verse* that Dylan Thomas was sufficiently aware of the central contribution of Freudian psychology to criticize it intelligently. It is also probable that he perused Jung's essay on "Psychology and Poetry" in the June 1930 issue of *transition*; his feminine characters spring from within the heroes, closely resembling the mother-sister-wife figures described by Jung as preexistent archetypes accompanied by symbolism of water and submersion.[32] Although one should not be tempted to apply Jung's psychological apparatus systematically to Thomas' work, there is no doubt that in his early prose he was trying to combine sexual and mythological patterns in a unique literary form. Eugene Jolas' editorship of *transition* was probably influential in Thomas' decision to construct personal myths: "We want myths and more myths!" Jolas declared in a flier to the June 1930 issue. It seems hardly coincidental that Thomas, who had already created a number of successful quasi-mythological tales, should have presented the psychologically complex dream story "The Mouse and the Woman" for publication in the 1936 issue.

It was during one of his visits to London between 1934 and 1936 that Dylan Thomas also made the acquaintance of Victor Neuburg, who had launched his career by awarding him the *Poet's Corner* prize of publication in March 1934. Neuburg, as Fitz-Gibbon recounts, had fallen "while at Cambridge in 1906, completely under the influence of Aleister Crowley, the self-styled magician who liked to be called the Great Beast or 666" and "who engaged in deplorable practices with assorted young men and women, talked in a queer semicockney accent, celebrated the black mass and generally larked about in a manner intended to scandalize the British public."[33] The discovery of the existence of such a person—who suggests to me a possible model for Charles Williams' Sir Giles Tumulty of *War in Heaven*—may have had more of an effect on Thomas' interest in witchcraft than more local sources.

The key year in Thomas' prewar or early writing seems to me to have been 1934, the year of the publication in December of *18 Poems*. After this first volume of lyrics, he began working over earlier drafts and turning them into such complicated poems as "Altarwise by owl-light" which evinces borrowing of images and figures from all sorts of esoteric sources. As Ralph Maud has strikingly illustrated, it was from the poetry notebooks of 1930–1934 that he drew the original compositions redrafted for *18 Poems* (1934), *Twenty-Five Poems* (1936), *The Map of Love* (containing most of the early prose as well as lyrics, in 1939), and even a few of the poems in *Deaths and Entrances* (1946).[34] Looking at his poetry as a whole, I find that he seems to have progressed from a natural or strongly sensual lyric of the pre-London days to a period of writing in which he was experimenting with surrealism, the occult, and whatever else his literary friends were talking about during those first heady visits to London. Whereas his prose made an abrupt shift from symbolism to realism after 1938, his period of dense, difficult verse gradually eased into a clearer but still richly symbolic style, such as that of "Ballad of the Long-legged Bait (1941), "Vision and Prayer" (1944), and "A Winter's Tale" (1945).

It was during 1934, the same year that he began experimenting with methods suggestive of surrealism (see Chapter 5), that Thomas copied into his Red Notebook all of the prose that he needed typed. This copybook, which has been carefully described by Donald Tritschler,[35] contains the titles of most of the published and a few of the unpublished early stories, pencilled on a map of Great Britain on the inside cover. The early prose represented in the manuscript and later published in *The Map of Love* (the American title was *The World I Breathe*) and *Adventures in the Skin Trade* describes, as Jacob Korg was the first to note, "a universe which mirrors man's spiritual trials by means of the pathetic fallacy. The poetic device which Thomas uses so effectively and which seemed so irrational to Ruskin has been justified by Freud and Bergson."[36] It is in the early poetry and prose that "the pathetic fallacy" governs Thomas' work most completely. The most subjective of his writing, the early work is given over to the recording of a personal struggle, of an attempt to come to terms with his own faculties, which provides both the latent narrative line and the thematic antithesis of each work. "If we try to discover what the poem is going to do for the poet," writes Burke, "we may discover a set of generalities as to what poems do for everybody."[37] This is not to say that only what Thomas *intended* a work to do provides an adequate analysis of its contents, nor to assert with Jung that the shape and content of a work of art is wholly determined by uncontrollable unconscious forces. We shall see in this study, particularly in Chapter 5, how a struggle between conscious and unconscious worlds takes place within many of the early tales and poems.

Although related in theme and imagery to the early poetry, the early prose is of course shaped according to the dictates of fiction. As I shall show in the following chapter, Thomas' unique fables are constructed out of a singular combination of personal and mythological materials. The protagonists, though very close to the author's personal point of view, are distanced sufficiently to progress upon adventures whose shape, obstacles, and goals provide clear frameworks for the accompanying symbolism and imagery. "The full significance of a poem," writes Maud, "will be in the literal narrative plus the central concept inherent in the symbolic power of the wording."[38] Many excellent studies of Thomas' poetry have been concerned with its wording, images, and symbols in their interrelationships, conflicts, and syntheses, while less attention has been paid to the "literal narrative" which bears an equal burden of delivery. It is in the early prose, of course, that such narrative patterns predominate, and it is my conviction that a study of the early tales is valuable not only in order to elucidate these neglected pieces, but also in order to cast light upon the narrative lines underlying much of the poetry.

As one reads more and more deeply into Dylan Thomas' prose and poetry—from the boyish encounters with woman and the devil in the 1930–1932 Notebook, through the strong, sensual lines of *18 Poems* and the complicated, exotic symbolism of "I, in my intricate image," "Grief thief of time," and particularly "Altarwise by owl-light," to the symbolic clarity of the later poems and finally to the plans for the Stravinsky postatomic opera—his themes and symbols begin to lose their eclecticism and fit together as parts of a fully developed personal universe. The chief end of this study thus goes beyond its special focus on the early prose, its ultimate purpose being the illumination of the strands of what seems a far more coherent poetic vision than has previously been attributed to Dylan Thomas' opus.

II

"Because Dylan was a very good writer certain academic critics, particularly in America, have endowed him with a profound knowledge of astronomy or theology, of Welsh metrics or even of biology, which he certainly did not possess," asserts FitzGibbon. "On the other hand . . . certain English academics . . . have denied that he was an original and important poet at all, though he certainly was."[39] What is it that motivates the American academics (myself among them) to endow the "untutored genius" with learning? Is it a perverse desire to endow an admired poet with the critic's own esoteric predilections? Or is it the effect of a puzzlingly coherent symbolic world out of which Dylan Thomas' works seem to be written? There has been a marked tendency among both English and American critics to conclude that Thomas was a first-rate poet in a limited number of cases—the author, for example, of four or five truly great poems of the critic's own choice. In the textual analysis that often precedes these conclusions, however, the critic like as not has noted parallels among symbols, images, or other figures and motifs in a number of individual poems, often enough taking note of a "symbolic universe" underlying a group of poems or even the total work. "The first and most striking unit of poetry larger than the individual poem," writes Northrop Frye, "is the total work of the man who wrote that poem."[40]

Even in such rigorously textual, word-by-word studies of each poem as William York Tindall's *A Reader's Guide to Dylan Thomas*, we often find the analysis of a given poem determined by a comparison between its images or motifs and those in other poems. In referring beyond the individual poem to the total work, Tindall implies that overall patterns of imagery and symbolism can contribute to the understanding of the individual poem. Ralph Maud's contribution to the field of Thomas criticism in his

Entrances to Dylan Thomas' Poetry is, like Tindall's, textual, and yet his classification of modes of composition goes one step further to an explicit analysis of Thomas' work as an opus. Maud casts considerable light upon the relationship between the narrative line of a poem and its constituent symbols or thematic imagery by describing their interaction in terms of structural categories. He devotes a chapter to an analysis of the prewar poems as "Process Poems" which "find their natural expression in antithetical imagery," and a later chapter to Thomas' method of "Distancing the Intimate" in his love poems, using "syntax as though it were a lock-gate, allowing meaning to come slowly through regulated compartments."[41] Maud seems to approach Thomas' methodology or "processes" as "symbolic actions" in the manner of Kenneth Burke, who has described works of literature in terms of "strategies," modes through which an author transforms personal situations into symbolic form.

In the area of source criticism Dr. Maud takes the position that references to Thomas' early readings are "of little use in illuminating any particular poem"; he takes up the question of specific sources only "because the negative answer supports what we instinctively feel about Thomas' poems: that they are new and unique, that no one wrote poems like these before, and that readers of Thomas have to begin without preconceptions."[42] Dr. Maud's intrinsic approach leads him nonetheless to a Freudian analogy: "one tussles with the intricacy of Thomas' imagery as Freud tackled dreams, but trusting that

the poet's creating, censoring, and selecting mind
has a responsibility and skill that the dreaming mind
does not."[43] Dr. Maud sees both critic and poet as
conscious, rational beings (in contrast to the Freudian patient who disguises the latent content of his
dream) wresting the raw materials of the unconscious into artistic order and form. However, even
though "Thomas must have known he was being
Freudian in certain places," Dr. Maud finds that the
"applicability of Freud to Thomas seems severely
limited."[44]

In Winifred Nowottny's explication of "There was
a Saviour" we find further conclusions on Thomas'
Freudianism. She describes "church," "wall," and
"rock" imagery as a thematic pattern in a number
of Thomas' poems and suggests an analogy to the
rock and prison imagery of William Blake. She also
notes that the progress of the poet's persona in
"There was a Saviour" takes a form suggestive of
Freudian patterns: "The necessary leap," she notes,
"is to the Freudian interpretation of the psyche.
(That is also, in a sense sufficiently approximate,
Blake's view of the psyche). In that interpretation,
people who have repressed their desires are always
so busy repressing them that they cut themselves off
from life as it might naturally be (cf. 'kept from the
sun')." Working from the text to the Freudian and
Blakean parallels, Miss Nowottny goes on to explain
that "we can hardly read the poem at all without
being conscious that it is going to relate its concerns
to what any reasonably sophisticated reader might
be expected to know about Freud. (Whether the

poet 'has a right' to take this knowledge for granted
is not my business to argue; I would argue only that
the poet does take it for granted)."[45]

It is surely somebody's business to decide whether
Thomas himself was "reasonably sophisticated"
enough to take Freudian theory for granted, and, if
he was, exactly how he came by his knowledge of
the psychoanalytic processes so keenly analyzed by
Miss Nowottny. "The fact that the dream is a compromise between conscious and unconscious states
serves both the analyst and the modern novelist,"
comments Frederick Hoffman in his definitive *Freudianism and the Literary Mind*.[46] It seems to me
that we need to reconsider at some depth just exactly how the dream serves Thomas in his tales of hallucination, madness, and dream. It is for this reason
that I have devoted a part of this biographical Introduction and the whole of Chapter 5 to a consideration of just how Thomas' symbolic and narrative
method might have been informed by contemporary
psychology. Similarly, I have devoted Chapter 4
to a study of how Blake's symbolic vision is reflected
in the early prose and poetry.

We must draw a further distinction between the
intrinsic, structural influence of dream or hallucination in Thomas' work (the influence, as Jung would
define it, of Thomas "collective unconscious") and
the influence of such extrinsic symbolic systems as
folklore, theology, and the occult. Given the critic's
understanding that textual evidence must be the
primary determinant of any influence on a given
poem or story, what is to be done when a symbol or

pattern of symbols bears marked resemblance to a symbol in a mythological, religious or occult source with which Thomas might have been familiar? Although few if any critics would impose their favorite esoterica upon an inappropriate text, certain of them have centered their analyses upon a correspondence between Thomas' symbols and material which might have been available to him but which they cannot prove that he read (see Appendix B). The pitfalls risked in dealing with such "sources" as Edward Davies and ab Ithel involve the danger of blurring two sets of critical distinctions: firstly, between probable and improbable sources for a given passage in Thomas' work (that is, between Thomas' use of a given figure and the critic's acquaintance with incidentally analogous figures); and, secondly, the distinction between conscious and unconscious influence, the question of whether the author deliberately picks symbols from conventional systems or whether such materials are presented to him inwardly, as it were, from the unconscious mind. We are on poor critical ground if there is nothing but an incidental analogy between a conventional symbol and an instance in the text. We are on shaky but not improper critical ground in assessing the influence of such folklore, theology, and occult lore as were probably present in Thomas' Welsh background, and we are on solid ground in such cases as Miss Nowottny's reference to Freud and Blake, whose systems in fact had some conscious influence on Thomas' literary method.

Our second critical problem leads us into the difficult and controversial realm of archetypal criticism, and here we must keep in mind four levels or worlds through which Thomas seems to move in both his prose and poetry: (1) the conscious level, where materials are available to him through his education, readings, and other conventional resources; (2) the preconscious level, defined by Bergson and Maritain as an intermediate realm between consciousness and unconsciousness sacred to the artist, who carries on the "preconscious life of the intellect" by absorbing conscious materials into unconscious ones, knitting them into art; (3) the level of the "personal" unconscious (as Jung described the Freudian unconscious), where impressions made during infancy mingle with other personal materials such as those engendered by one's family and sexual experiences; and (4) the collective unconscious (as defined by Jung), where simply as a human being the poet shares in the universally recurrent symbols and myths of the race.[47] These distinctions would of course be superfluous if they did not inform the narrative pattern of Thomas' prose tales. His heroes often move down through the preconscious preoccupations of the poet or artist and through a world of familiar and personal imagery to a penultimate adventure which bears the characteristics of a myth or a dream.

"Certain groups of decadents found it easier to imitate De Quincey's opium than his eloquence," remarks G. K. Chesterton, and I suppose that it is easier for literary critics to take the archetypal categories explored by Jung and Frye as a systematic canon than as the flexible critical tools for which

they are useful. To Frye the archetype is simply a
"smaller unit" than plot, perhaps such a leitmotif as
the dark and light heroines in Hawthorne's *Marble
Faun*.[48] An analogy between these heroines and the
dark and light antinomies of primitive religion is interesting but not necessarily helpful; a reference to
the way that they determine the structure of Hawthorne's plot (in a manner perhaps analogous to
their interaction in the religion or folklore in question) is both interesting and textually helpful. That
many of the landscapes, symbolic antitheses, and
mythological narratives of Thomas' early prose bear
analogy to the reputed "druid lore" is interesting;
the value of Chapters 2 and 3 of this study must be
determined by the extent to which the analogy
elucidates the texts in question and casts light, in
turn, upon Thomas' total work.

The central determinant of any interpretation of
Thomas' or any other body of literature must thus
be the text, as it is composed of images, metaphors,
and symbols which occur not as isolated tokens
dropped from the mysterious heavens of conventional symbologies but as parts of a total symbolic construct which is the work of art itself. He who best
understands Thomas' total work is the one who com-
prehends the individual poems and tales in terms
of the images, symbols, and themes that interact
within them. The dangers of source criticism should
not, however, prohibit critical ventures into the
tricky waters of influence; this critic, for one, prefers
to risk laughter from the grave could we be brought
closer to an understanding of the unique symbolic
universe underlying Thomas' works.

CHAPTER I

The Structure of the Early Prose

"The union of ritual and dream in the form of verbal communication is myth."

> *Northrop Frye,* Anatomy of Criticism

I

Dylan Thomas never typed his own stories for submission to periodicals, but he would copy the finished version in careful handwriting into the Red Notebook, from which he would dictate to a friend. Reading aloud was as important for the prose as for the poetry, and many stories were tried out before a group of friends during the Wednesday lunch hour in Swansea. In the same manner "The Enemies," "The Visitor," "The Orchards," "The Mouse and the Woman," and "The Burning Baby" were read aloud, mainly during 1934, to Pamela Hansford Johnson.[1]

Although from 1934 on many of the tales were published in Welsh and English periodicals, Thomas was as concerned with bringing them together into one volume as he was with publishing collections of his poems. By 1937 he had assembled the major early tales in *The Burning Baby* and had contracted with the Europa Press for publication. It was already advertised and the first edition subscribed when the printers balked on grounds of obscenity. A depressing back and forth of compromise and argument ensued, and, as the efforts of George Reavey of the Europa Press proved unavailing, Thomas began to toy with the idea of publishing the tales through Lawrence Durrell and Henry Miller in Paris (several stories, including "A Prospect of the Sea," were eventually translated in *l'Arche* by Francis Dufeu-L'Abeyrie). When the situation became hopeless Reavey turned the contract over to the Pearn, Pollinger, and Higham literary agency. Their good offices also proved useless, and although "In the Direction of the Beginning" found its way into a New Directions collection and several other stories were printed in *The Map of Love* and *The World I Breathe* (England and America, 1939), *The Burning Baby* never went to press.

The suppression of the early tales and the poor reception of the volumes that combined poetry and prose may have accounted in part for the abrupt change in prose style that occurred throughout 1938 and 1939. This was also, of course, a time of impending war when the outer world was pressing in upon Thomas as upon everyone else. The early prose tales were part of an inward universe that he constructed in his late teens and early twenties: the war not only disrupted this universe but afforded Thomas the opportunity of trying his hand at the more public genres of broadcasting and "straight" narrative fiction. The early prose tales are much more a unity with the poetry than the later, more simplistic *Portrait of the Artist as a Young Dog* (1940) and "Adventures in the Skin Trade" (1941), which Thomas himself tended to deprecate. Although the late Vernon Watkins disagreed with me entirely, thinking that "Dylan always did what he wanted to do, in spite of the success or failure of his work,"[2] I think that with his pressing financial needs at that time he could not afford to write in a prose genre that had been poorly received by both printers and public.

The early prose was not collected until after Thomas' death: the two posthumous volumes, *A Prospect of the Sea* (England) and *Adventures in the Skin Trade* (America), did not appear until 1955.[3] At that time they were often invidously compared to the later prose (*Portrait of the Artist as a Young Dog* and *Under Milk Wood*) which had become popular and even beloved. American critics reserved judgement on the "poetic" and "difficult" pieces following "Adventures in the Skin Trade."[4] But Davies Aberpennar in Wales and Kingsley Amis in England had already found them irresponsibly irrational, full of "factitious surrealist artifice," and built upon "characters and situations . . . which people in full possession of their faculties would not find interesting or important."[5] Many admirers of the early poetry consigned the early prose to oblivion as juvenilia, or dismissed it as part of a macabre or dark phase which was as well forgotten. To G. S.

Fraser they were the "pièces noires" of Thomas' later "celebration of innocence." Fraser insists that "in writing these pieces, Thomas was grappling with, and apparently succeeded in absorbing and overcoming, what Jungians call the shadow."[6]

Such an opinion overlooks Thomas' lifelong bout with a "shadow" which he never overcame. The life of the poet, wrote Jung in the June 1930 *transition*, "is, of necessity, full of conflicts, since two forces fight in him: the ordinary man with his justified claim for happiness . . . , and the ruthless creative passion on the other which under certain conditions crushes all personal desires into the dust."[7] Throughout the forties Thomas was caught in the toils of just such a conflict, and he devoted neither his later poetry nor his later prose to gay reminiscence. Perhaps the critics of the fifties were looking for their own prewar innocence in suggesting that the stories of *Portrait of the Artist as a Young Dog*, the short novel "Adventures in the Skin Trade," or the drama *Under Milk Wood* were visions of an unsullied, dirty-little-boy Eden. Like Blake's, Thomas' vision of innocence was through the eyes of experience.

Dylan Thomas was certainly not alone among twentieth-century writers in regarding madness, dream, and myth as a fertile source of imagery and narrative material. His tales are concerned with how the storyteller breaks from the bounds of consciousness into the unconscious world, what he experiences there, how he manages to return, and what happens if he does not return (Marlais takes something resembling a psychedelic "trip" in "The Orchards," as does Peter in "The Visitor" and Nant in "The Lemon"). The inward journey of the poetic imagination, which is usually implicit in the poetry, is more explicit in the prose, where it is *the* adventure by which Thomas self-consciously defines his narrative mode.

Even though the symbolic forms of the unconscious provide both the goal of his heroes and the structure of his tales, he is careful that the unconscious world never usurps control of the narrative. As we shall see in Chapter 5, the only passages of "automatic writing" in the tales occur when Thomas wants to describe the abrogation of consciousness: he seems to have felt that the further inward the narrative penetrates, the stronger must be the role played by the intellect. "The more subjective a poem," he wrote, "the clearer the narrative line."[8] The intense and often hallucinatory subjectivity of the early tales required an unusual amount of conscious control, and it is probably for this reason that Thomas intruded so often as omniscient narrator. As Jacob Korg has noted, he shapes paranoia and hallucination into "an atmosphere where the mind rules the material world, exercising its powers of creation and distortion over it."[9]

II

The "progressive line, or theme, or movement" which Thomas insisted upon for every poem is also present in every tale, where it is defined by the progress of the hero from desire through quest to release and renewal. The plots are divided into three or four sections which succeed each other with the rhythm of ritual movements. The tales usually culminate in a sacrament or rite, an act of sexual release, or an archetypal vision. The release may take the form of the loosing of a flood (as in "A Prospect of the Sea" and "The Map of Love") or of an apocalyptic event ("The Holy Six," "An Adventure from a Work in Progress," "The Visitor"). Often the beginning of a new epoch of search and birth is implicit in the cataclysmic denouement, giving a cyclical shape to the narrative.

William York Tindall includes "landscape and sea, enclosures such as garden, island, and cave, and in addition city and tower" under the category of archetype. He goes on to explain that "uniting the personal and the general and commonly ambivalent, these images, not necessarily symbolic in themselves, become symbolic by context, first in our sleeping minds and then in poems."[10] Thomas' landscapes embody the personal or sexual, the impersonal or mythical, and the poetic aspirations of his heroes. Images of the poetic quest seem to rise up as autonomous entities out of the countryside: words become incarnate in trees, in blood, and in the transforming sea. Often, at the denouement of a tale, they find their final expression in a "voice of thunder" which announces the hero's achievement.

Since Thomas' landscape is not only geographical but anatomical, personal or sexual imagery is latent in the countryside as well as in the bodies of hero and heroine. The hills and valleys of "A Prospect of the Sea," "The Map of Love," the two fragments ("In the Direction of the Beginning" and "An Adventure from a Work in Progress"), and "The Holy Six" are metaphors of the feminine anatomy, the breasts, belly, and so forth, of the earth-mother herself. In "The Map of Love" the map which Sam Rib explicates is of sexual intercourse: the island "went in like the skin of lupus to his touch. . . . Here seed, up the tide, broke on the boiling coasts; the sand grains multiplied" (*AST*, p. 146). In the tales where the cyclical pattern is most pronounced the feminine landscape is itself circular, dominated by a woman who draws the hero into the "mothering middle of the earth." In "In the Direction of the Beginning," "An Adventure from a Work in Progress," "The Enemies," and "The Holy Six," the heroes walk from the rim of an island or valley through ancestral fields into intercourse. Each consummation is analogous to a mythological event, during which the island or circular valley participates in an orgy of division and regeneration. As Dr. Maud has aptly pointed out, Thomas' mingling of geographic and sexual imagery is a successful method of "distancing the intimate," a means of describing the act of love so that both its intimate and mythical qualities are dramatically embodied.[11]

Neither the aesthetic imagery, which expresses the poetic quest of the hero, nor the sexual imagery of a given tale predominates. In each case poetic and anatomical metaphors describe a narrative line which is essentially mythological, both in the inward sense ("the union of ritual and dream in the form of verbal communication") and in the outward or historical sense (the use of Welsh, Egyptian, and other folklore for background). The final synthesis is always personal: images describing the heroes' thrust towards sexual and poetic maturity are overlaid by thematic antitheses of unity and division, love and death. "Poetry in its social or archetypal aspect," notes Frye, "not only tries to illustrate the fulfillment of desire, but to define the obstacles to it. Ritual is not only a recurrent act, but an act expressive of a dialectic of desire and repugnance: desire for fertility or victory, repugnance to draught or to enemies."[12] We shall see how demonic vitality and senile repression form the poles of "The Enemies" and "The Holy Six"; in "The Mouse and the Woman" and "The Map of Love" we shall find heroes suspended between fear of the flesh and sensual desire.

"If ritual is the cradle of language," declares Suzanne Langer, "metaphor is the law of its life."[13] Thomas' narratives depend upon the conflict, mergence, and progression of specific metaphors. Given the analogy of geography and anatomy which underlies most of the early tales, even his descriptive images bear a metaphorical burden. In "The Burning Baby," for example, the relationship between images of gorse, flesh, and fire marks the progression of the plot towards its grim crescendo. At the outset, Thomas describes Rhys Rhys preaching a sermon on "The beauty of the harvest" and explains that in the preacher's mind "it was not the ripeness of God that glistened from the hill. It was the promise and the ripeness of the flesh, the good flesh, the mean flesh, flesh of his daughter, flesh, flesh, the flesh of the voice of thunder howling before the death of man" (*AST*, p. 91). The biblical metaphor of flesh to grass is the raw material of Rhys' perversion. It embodies both the sensual level ("the flesh of his daughter") and the poetic level ("the flesh of the voice of thunder") of the plot.

Further on in the tale a third element is added to the metaphor: the little brother "saw the high grass at [his sister's] thighs. And the blades of the up-growing wind, out of the four windsmells of the manuring dead, might drive through the soles of her feet, up the veins of the legs and stomach, into her womb and her pulsing heart" (*AST*, p. 93). The grass has become an even more explicitly sexual metaphor, each blade being analogous to the father's phallus. The "upgrowing wind" surging through the grass is in turn analogous to the spirit, both as the biblical wind which "bloweth where it listeth" and as the impregnator of Mary. Coming into conjunction with flesh the fiery biblical wind ignites as the elements of gorse, flesh, wind, and fire merge in the burning baby. The denouement is organic, in the sense of propounding a natural, season-oriented or cyclical worldview. Rhys Rhys sets fire to the gorse to burn the incestuously begotten son as the tale concludes, its final scene a variation on Abraham's sacrifice of Isaac, God's sacrifice of Christ, and man's perennial sacrifice of himself.

"The Burning Baby" is a fairly early and straightforward tale from the Red Notebook in September, 1934. We shall see in Chapter 5 how, in "The Mouse and the Woman," "The Lemon," and "The Orchards," Thomas uses images from a series of related dreams to underline the narrative. In the tales where there is no dreaming he makes use of a similar mode of metaphorical progression. For each of the three key characters of "The Enemies" and "The Holy Six," the world shapes itself into images appropriate to his perception of it. Mr. Owen is a kind of Great-Uncle Jarvis, a lover of the "vegetable world" that "roared under his feet." Endowing his garden with his own virility, he works upon the "brown body of the earth, the green skin of the grass, and the breasts of the Jarvis hills." Mrs. Owen's feminine powers are embodied in her crystal ball, which contains the extremities of hot and cold, clarity and obscurity and is analogous both to her womb and to the round earth whirling outside of the house. Davies, withered with age and insubstantial with sterility, perceives the Jarvis valley as a place of demonic vitality, death, and nausea. Throughout the narrative, it remains a "great grey green earth" that "moved unsteadily beneath him."

Ghostliness, virility, and demonic lust are embodied in Davies' nausea, Owen's garden, and Mrs. Owen's crystal ball. As the narrative moves towards its consummation the action moves entirely indoors to concentrate upon the ball and Mrs. Owen's pregnant womb. The six clergymen are made to share in Davies' nausea, vomiting up their desires under the influence of "mustard and water." At the denouement the conflict centers upon a question of paternity: whose child is in Mrs. Owen's womb? Ghostliness triumphs as Davies is assured that he has not loved Amabel in vain. As Owen, like Callaghan, laughs that there should "be life in the ancient loins," Davies sees "the buried grass shoot through the new night and move on the hill wind." Mr. Owen is revealed as the midwife-gardener to Mrs. Owen and Davies, laboring to bring new life out of a woman who conceives only in the arms of death. The antithetical metaphors of virility and ghostliness are woven into a new synthesis by Mrs. Owen's paradoxical desires. The narrative as a whole is a symbolic representation of an apocalyptic union of spirit and flesh, the dead and the living.

So intensely does Thomas concentrate upon a metaphor to make it render its utmost significance that his figures nearly burst their usual function, no longer representing a similarity but a metamorphosis. It is as if he, like his heroes, could change real objects into their subjective equivalents, and elements of the outer world into his lyric image of them. Thus in "A Prospect of the Sea" the boy sees a tree turn into the countryside: "every leaf of the tree that shaded them grew to man-size then, the ribs of the bark were channels and rivers wide as a great ship; and the moss on the tree, and the sharp grass ring round the base, were all the velvet covering of a green country's meadows blown hedge to hedge" (AST, p. 127). By a process similar to hallucination the objects of the landscape become elements of a subjective vision, the tree on the hill becoming a symbolic expression of the boy's own transformation.

"The chief source of obscurity in these stories," remarks Jacob Korg, "is the fact that imagined things are expressed in the language of factual statement instead of the language of metaphor."[14] Thus when Thomas writes of the girl in "A Prospect of the Sea" that "the heart in her breast was a small red bell that rang in a wave," one cannot comprehend the metaphor until one accepts the previous statement that the waves not only resemble but *are* a "white-faced sea of people, the terrible mortal number of the waves, all the centuries' sea drenched in the hail before Christ" (*AST*, p. 131). The girl herself *is* a wave, her heart a meeting place of men and mermen, land and sea. If the sea is a metaphor of the human race, it is what Tindall has termed a "metaphysical metaphor," symbolic in itself and an "element of a symbolic structure."[15]

Thomas' "metaphysical metaphors" are thematic symbols embodying the progression and antitheses upon which such a narrative depends. They are not literary tokens heightening realistic situations in the classic sense, nor are they incorporated into the tales from an external system. Within each story, they are distinguished from minor metaphors by the way that they juxtapose, blend, and contain the several dominant themes. The tree in "The Tree," "A Prospect of the Sea," and "The Orchards"; the house in "The Enemies," "The Holy Six" and "The Dress"; and the tower in "The Lemon" and "The School for Witches" are such inclusive symbols.

None of them is the only major symbol in its context, however. Tree, tower, and house form a symbolic triad in "The Tree"; orchard, scarecrow, and maiden are one among several such triads in "The Orchards," while house, hill, and sea contain the thematic meaning of "The Mouse and the Woman" and "A Prospect of the Sea."

In each tale, objects contract and expand, merge and reshape themselves according to the pressure of the hero's mind. Like a magician, the poet-hero forces the image of a thing to become the thing itself. Although he draws upon the worlds of magic, folk belief, and madness for his material, Thomas exercises careful control over it, subordinating it to the expression of the hero's quest for meaning. Discontented with images and metaphors that are merely literary and decorative, the hero condemns the "dead word," story-princesses, and conventional metaphors, forcing himself into the dangerous world of the unconscious where symbols are live things which devour as they illuminate. Since the stories are about the search for a source of all story the symbolic visions which mark each denouement are ends in themselves.

III

It is a pity that there are no recordings of the early tales, which Thomas read aloud during the Wednesday lunch hours to his Swansea friends and, in London, to Pamela Hansford Johnson and her mother at 53 Battersea Rise. For all of its wordiness Thomas' prose style is extremely symmetrical, with orderly paragraphs progressing according to the dictates of balance and emphasis.

The texts alternate between lengthy descriptive passages, briefer paragraphs which sum up the descriptions or outline further action, and brief dialogues. Even in the longer descriptive sections there is a great deal of activity, the prose bristling with verbs of action and reaction describing the thematic conflict. Thomas often relies upon a series of clauses or phrases which he builds into a crescendo at the climax of a passage. In "A Prospect of the Sea" one paragraph begins with a brief and realistic statement: "It was hot that morning in the unexpected sunshine. A girl dressed in cotton put her mouth to his ear," and continues

Along the bright wrackline, from the horizon where the vast birds sailed like boats, from the four compass corners, bellying up through the weed-beds, melting from orient and tropic, surging through the ice hills and the whale grounds, through sunset and sunrise corridors, the salt gardens and the herring fields, whirlpool and rock pool, out of the trickle in the mountain, down the waterfalls, a white-faced sea of people. . . . (*AST*, pp. 130–31)

The participial series, "bellying," "melting," "surging," gives way to a series of adverbial phrases which finally find their subject at the middle of the paragraph. The prose catalogue suggests a sweeping up and down of the earth, a gathering of the "white-faced sea of people" from the north and south, the east and west.

Passages so rich and lengthy generally occur only

near the climax of the tales. Thomas leads up to them with shorter paragraphs, composed of a simple sentence at the beginning and end and one or two more complex sentences in between. Brief statement, mounting descriptive rhythms, and brevity of concluding statement are the basic units not only of individual paragraphs but of each story as a whole. Each tale begins and ends with a simplicity which must take its significance from the complex material in between. In nearly every case the plot is rounded out with some such simple statement as

Hold my hand, he said. And then: Why are you putting the sheet over my face? ("The Visitor")

or

Brother, he said. He saw that the child held silver nails in the palm of his hand. ("The Tree")

or

Cool rain began to fall. ("A Prospect of the Sea")

Thomas' dialogues are constructed along similar lines, occurring not as conventional conversations but as catechetical interchanges which usually precede or follow a complex and lengthy description. In "The Visitor" the paragraphs describing the arrival of Peter and Callaghan in the land of death are followed by this interchange:

What is this valley? said Peter's voice.
The Jarvis valley, said Callaghan. Callaghan, too, was dead. Not a bone or a hair stood up under the steadily falling frost.
This is no Jarvis valley.
This is the naked valley. (*AST*, p. 82–83)

From this dialogue, resembling that of God and Ezekiel in the valley of dry bones, the reader is flung on into the powerful description of the deluge of blood which causes even the "monstrous nostrils of the moon" to widen in horror. In "The Tree," similarly, the description of the boy's view of the Jarvis valley is followed by his question and the gardener's answer:

Who are they, who are they?
They are the Jarvis hills, said the gardener, which have been from the beginning. (*AST*, p. 75)

A variation of the catechetical dialogue appears in the riddling interchanges that summarize the paradoxical themes of "The Horse's Ha" and "In the Direction of the Beginning." These bring the reader to a stop and make him, like the hero, puzzle over the significance of the adventure, giving him a pause for reflection before he is plunged into ever more complex prose. Thomas possibly derived this technique from the rhetoric of Welsh preachers.

No study of the metaphorical or rhetorical structure of Thomas' prose can explain its weirdly compelling lilt, indescribable except by reading the tales aloud. This lilt is more pronounced in the shorter paragraphs and depends upon delicate balance of sentence elements. It is not original to Thomas, who may have modeled his prose after the style of Caradoc Evans.[16] Take Thomas' description of Amabel Owen: "She was a tidy little body, with plump hands and feet, and a love-curl glistened on her forehead; dressed, like a Sunday, in cold and shining black, with a brooch of mother's ivory and a bone-white bangle, she saw the Holy Six reflected as six solid stumps . . ." (*AST*, p. 136), and compare it with a passage from Evans: "Silah Schoolen was a tidy bundle and she was dressed as if every day was a Sunday. She was not tall or short, fat or thin; her cheekbones were high and her lips were wide and her top teeth swelled from her mouth in a snowy white arch."[17] In Evans the lilt derives from the adaptation into English of the rhythms of spoken Welsh. Modified slightly by Thomas, it is present in combination with a terse descriptive economy in most of his early tales.

Although Evans' use of dialogue is more conventional and extensive than that of Thomas, Evans relies upon a similar combination of catechism and proverb:

"And who is the husband shall I say?"
"He was Shacki. O you heard of Shacki—Shacki stallion?"
"I have been in ships," said the man. "I have been with black heathens and whites Holy Sherusalem [sic]."
"The Sea is a stormy place. Have you rabbits to sell?"
Amos made this pronouncement: "There are no rabbits on tidy farms."[18]

Where Evans' prose is full of folk proverb, Thomas is more likely to invent proverbial statements from a combination of Welsh mythology, Christianity, and the sexual metaphors of a given story. Thus where one of Evans' heroes asserts that "Death is a great stiffener," Thomas asserts that "No drug of man works on the dead. The parson, at his pipe,

sucked down a dead smoke." Evans' tales are terse
and economical descriptions of the realistic tragedies
of the country, Hardyesque in their reliance upon
local dialogue and superstition. Usually curling into
a bitter twist at the denouement, they are far more
like Joyce's *Dubliners* than Thomas' early prose.

Although Evans is likely to start a story with a
statement like "A tree of wisdom grew inside a certain farmer and sayings fell from it," he usually goes
on to more realistic statements. Thomas is more
likely to start out realistically and to become more
and more fantastic. In this he certainly owes something to the influence of T. F. Powys. In *Mockery
Gap*, for example, Powys endows the sea with much
the same powers of love and regeneration as Thomas
does in such tales as "The Map of Love" and "A
Prospect of the Sea": "Mr. Pattimore sat up. He
heard the midnight sea, the wicked one, the beautiful, the inspirer of huge wickedness; he heard the
sea. However much he had shut out from him all
the gentle longings of his loving lady, the sound
would come in. It came from the dark places of
love, out of the bottom of the sea."[19] In *The Innocent Birds* the landscape suggests that of "The Map
of Love": the hero, "old Solly," overhearing two lovers on the "green summit" of the focal Madder Hill,
associates them with the creative and destructive
potentialities of the sea beneath them.

In Powys' *The Two Thieves* we find a macabre
turn of events expressed in a style similar to that of
Thomas' darker tales: "Grace crept into a corner of
the room. She already felt the serpent growing in

her womb. She tried to tear open her body with her nails: in three weeks she was measured for her coffin. The undertaker had expected her to be a little taller than she was. 'A beautiful corpse,' he said smilingly."[20] Powys' tales are structured upon the organic cyclical pattern beloved to Thomas: "Every Autumn God dies," he writes in *God*, "and in the spring He is given a new place in the lives of men, and is born again. It is the same with us; we die and go down to the pit, but until the worlds vanish, new life from our dust will arise and worship the sun."[21]

"The quality and organization of the language here," writes one commentator, "is poetic in its deep rhythms and its surface music."[22] Thomas once described his early prose as "this bastard thing, a prose-poetry."[23] Although his tales do not belong in the French genre of the *poème en prose* favored by Max Jacob and André Breton, in style and form they somewhat resemble such "prose-poems" as Rimbaud's *Illuminations* (compare "Après le Deluge" to "The Map of Love," "Villes" to "Prologue to an Adventure" and Lautrémont's "Les Chants de Maldoror"). In England as in France the two separate genres of prose and poetry merged in the experimental novel of the twenties and thirties. While Anna Balakian notes in surrealist France "a fusion of poetry with prose,"[24] Professor Tindall has aptly pointed out that in England, at the same time, "the better novel became a poem" with its "narrative and subordinate details centered in image."[25]

Thomas' early tales, as we have seen, are "poetic"

in their dependence upon a balance, progression, and contrast of thematic images and symbols. They differ from the work of Woolf, Lawrence, and Joyce, however, not only in their brevity but in their intense subjectivism. Where the other novelists create a number of distinct characters upon whose minds the outer world registers its impressions, Thomas' tales more often center upon one protagonist. Even when a consort, father-figure or antagonist is present he or she is absorbed, in the end, into an inward or personal vision. (The triad of Mrs. Owen, Mr. Owen, and Davies in "The Enemies" is a notable exception to this practice.) When a number of persons are involved, as in "The Horse's Ha" and "The School for Witches," they all are absorbed into a demonic or ritual unity at the denouement. Thomas thus pays little heed to Stephen Daedalus' plea for dramatic distancing over lyric subjectivism, for the conflict within each tale is less between separate persons than between the hero's Blakean faculties of imagination, reason, and desire.

Thomas' tales are not as dependent upon conflicting and merging images as are his poems. Narrative is fundamental to their structures in which action and images are knit together with careful attention to plot coherence and rhetorical style. The result is a genre unique in contemporary fiction, which in its pattern of quest for a fabulous center is more like folktale or mythological legend than realistic fiction. In each story, the protagonist sways between moods of approach and withdrawal which shape the narrative into a strophic and antistrophic "dancing of an attitude."[26]   In such stories as "The Enemies," "The Holy Six," "The Orchards," "The Map of Love," "A Prospect of the Sea," "The Lemon," and "The School for Witches," the protagonists move through a ritual series of trials and adventures towards the paradoxical goal of vision and destruction.   In others, such as "The Horse's Ha," "The Tree," and "The Burning Baby," a similar ritual movement, sometimes circling, sometimes progressing, embodies a dance of death and renewal.

Each of Thomas' early tales contains elements of myth (pseudo-primitive folklore or inward ritual), theology (in the sense of a system of cosmic symbology, containing—but transcending—myth), the occult (heretical materials combining the primitive and organic with the transcendent) and, finally, surrealism (the contemporary practice of mingling unconscious, mythological and everyday images into a new, hallucinatory or super-real world view).   In each story these elements are knit carefully into an artistic whole, and it might seem a violation of the artistic integrity of each piece to separate its various components, in the following chapters.   Only the casual reader should be thrown off by this deliberate unravelling, however.   The intent is to elucidate the various strands of Thomas' early prose style so that the reader, winding these strands back together in his perusal of the individual tales, will more fully grasp their richness.

Certain stories seem to illustrate one of the four influences better than others, and it is for this reason that, in each chapter, I have concentrated on three to five particular stories to explain my hypothesis. In Chapter 2, "The Map of Love," "A Prospect of the Sea," "In the Direction of the Beginning," "An Adventure from a Work in Progress," and "The Orchards" are exemplars of Thomas' use of the folklore of island, voyage, flood and sun. In Chapter 3, "The Visitor," "The Orchards," "The Tree," and the unpublished "Gaspar, Melchior, Balthasar" are used to explain Thomas' unique religion. In Chapter 4 "The Enemies," "The Holy Six," "The School for Witches," and "The Horse's Ha" help us in our comprehension of the organic or occult tradition in Thomas' tales, while surrealism plays a predominant part in "The Lemon," "The Orchards," and "The Mouse and the Woman," in Chapter 5. Finally, Chapter 6 contains an analysis of "Adventures in the Skin Trade" as well as a brief review of the stories in *Portrait of the Artist as a Young Dog*.

CHAPTER II

Mythology in the Early Prose

"Three things that enrich the poet: Myths, poetic power, a store of ancient verse."

The Red Book of Hergest

I

Dylan Thomas' early fiction, like much of his poetry and later prose, is built upon the contrast of innocence and experience. From the universal and embarrassing agonies of puberty he forges presentations of ritual initiation into manhood that achieve the style and stature of myth. By "myth" I mean, in this context, both the social, pseudohistorical folklore handed down through tradition and the inward, integrative symbolism which the individual shapes into art. The relationship between the external-historical and internal-creative mythological worlds was described by Jung in the June 1930 issue of *transition*: "It is . . . entirely logical that the poet should return to the mythological figure (or at least to pseudo-history) in order to find a fitting expression for his experience. Nothing would be more erroneous than to assume that the poet creates from the material of tradition, he works rather from the primal experience, the dark nature of which requires mythological figures and thus draws avidly to itself everything that is akin, to be used for self expression."[1]

For the purpose of elucidating the symbols and narratives in Dylan Thomas' early prose I will be making a distinction between mythology, as primitive or pseudoprimitive narrative; theology, as myth incorporated into (and therefore legitimized within) a systematic, religious symbology; and the occult, the bastard result of the survival of mythology into the period of a new theology. Since myth is apt to be the disreputable ancestor of new theologies and all theologies are replete with tags of myth, the distinction between the present chapter and that following might appear arbitrary: there are, however, *both* mythological and theological phases in the pre-Christian Welsh materials that bear upon Thomas' prose. The reader must judge for himself whether the separation of the more primitive, fragmentary influences from those more systematic and theological is helpful.

Folk legends and myths that survive into a new historical-religious period, since they are survivals of a more primitive or organic worldview, are likely to be singled out for particular animosity by the newly orthodox. Throughout the Middle Ages and the Renaissance (as Frazer and Campbell have illustrated)[2] such primitive cults were never far below the surface of European orthodoxy, persisting "underground" and recondite with coded symbologies. Should a group of initiates separate themselves from the dominant religion they would be burned, hunted, and persecuted as heretics and witches. Nonetheless persistent, the occult, Kabbalistic, and witch "cults" of Europe have remained active until the present day, mingling primitive materials with more sophisticated rites of worship. We will consider the possible influence of these systems upon Dylan Thomas' early prose in Chapter 4.

Ever since Thomas Hardy, George Moore, the naturalists, decadents, and atheists released themselves from the last shreds of the pre-Darwinian worldview there has been a restoration of both primitive mythology and its occult derivatives in literature, as if human nature abhorred a vacuum. One of the predominant characteristics of T. S. Eliot, James Joyce, D. H. Lawrence, Hart Crane, William Carlos Williams, Saul Bellow, John Updike, and any number of contemporary writers has been their reformulation of myth, theology, and the occult, not as interesting anachronistic tags but as intrinsic elements in their works.

Just such a "creative mythology," structured out of a new, personal synthesis, undergirds Dylan Thomas' total work.[3] My concern is to reveal the integrity of this synthesis by an exploration of various possible sources for its elements and of the way in which they seem knit together in the early prose. Whether, in Thomas' case, they are drawn from a self-conscious perusal of ancient texts or from his own personal pilgrimage is a matter secondary to my concern with the role of mythological figures in the unity of his vision.

II

Welsh mythology, which like other mythologies consists of imaginative narratives bolstered by a residuum of history, is far less familiar to the reader of today than is the folklore of Greece and Rome. In England, where in Caesar's time the continental druids journeyed to find their ancient lore preserved in its purest form, the classical tongues rather than any indigenous British language have been studied as the taproots of civilization.

Although druid archaeology is almost intangible, the origin and nature of druid religious practices uncertain, and druid history often a matter of literary romanticizing—from the first cleric to syncretize pagan and Christian materials to Robert Graves' labors on *The White Goddess*—druids, bards, and Welsh epic heroes have excited perennial conjecture. The English poets, comments A. L. Owen in *The Famous Druids*, "all have some odd things to say of the Druids: Drayton's are drawn through the air by dragons; Milton calls on Parliament to follow the example of the Druids; Pope's Druids may be taken for Scythian heroes; Marvell and Wordsworth picture themselves as Druids, Collins calls Thomson a Druid, and Blake calls Adam a Druid."[4] Thomas, singing by the coffin of his Aunt Ann Jones as "druid of her broken body," stands in a long tradition of literary adoption of druids for personal, poetic ends.

The history of Welsh mythology is not entirely speculative, however, as there are several good sources of information about the pre-Christian and early Christian inhabitants of Wales: first, such classical writers as Caesar, Pliny, Tacitus, and Strabo; then, the apparently genuine ancient texts compiled in the *Myverian Archaelogy of Wales*; the Celtic researches of such anthropological scholars as Frazer and Joseph Campbell; and, finally, such excellent essays in literary history as those of R. S. Loomis' *Wales and the Arthurian Legend*.

In *Occidental Mythology* Campbell describes a Cymric or La Tène culture which overthrew the earlier, more primitive bronze and stone age populations of Wales and Ireland during the fifth century B.C. The earlier cultures were not entirely lost, as tags and pieces of their legends continued to pass down orally among the subjugated population, eventually permeating the poems that form the content of *The Black Book of Carmarthen* (c. A.D. 1200), the *Red Book of Hergest* (c. 1400), and Owen Jones' compilation, the *Myverian Archaelogy of Wales* (1801–1807). Nor were the pre-Cymric peoples lost to literary history: they became the tall, silver-haired Tuatha de Danaan ("the children of the Goddess Dana, who retired, when defeated, into wizard hills of glass").[5] These Irish fairies were restored to modern literature by the efforts of John O'Leary, Lady Gregory, Yeats, and the Irish Nationalists early in the twentieth century: their labyrinthine granges, spirals, and gyres appear in the symbolism of the Vorticists, and of Joyce and Yeats.

Arthur Machen, determined to restore dignity to the "aboriginals" of Wales, argues that they became known as "little people" (witness Shakespeare's

Puck and Ariel) because, forced to live nomadically on a low protein diet, they actually became diminished in stature. J. R. R. Tolkien has seen to it that they are restored to normal size (taller than average European—perhaps average American) in his epic saga, *The Lord of the Rings*, where both the adventures and the language (Elvish) of the fairy nobility have been systematically recreated.

We learn from Caesar that such Celts as the Brythonic Cymri who invaded Wales and the Goidelic Cymri who overthrew the Danaans divided themselves into two aristocratic castes: the druids and the knights. The knights practiced a highly successful warfare (they held Rome itself in thrall in 390 B.C.) while the druids held aloof from battle, gathering pupils about them to memorize quantities of verse and to be instructed "touching the stars and their movements, the size of the universe, and of the earth, the order of nature, the strength and powers of the immortal gods."[6] They taught that men's souls were indestructible, passing at death into new incarnations according to their previous life. Fire, sun, and stars were part of their astronomical worship: they constructed sophisticated temples to the sun, perhaps influenced, as Graves suggests, by the Chaldean mode of worship in an eastern land of origin.

Druid poetry was as closely linked to science as druid knowledge to political power. The result was an aristocratic tradition in letters by which in Ireland the druids provided court poets (known as ollaves) who were second in honor only to the

queen; and in Wales the court druids (called bards)
were "possessed of a professional tradition, embodied in a corpus of poems which, literally memorized and carefully weighed, they passed on to the
pupils who came to study under them."[7] The Welsh
bards were no less politically powerful than their
Irish cousins: according to Robert Graves, they
made a serious attempt to prevent a revival of the
folklore of the ragged popular ministrels whom they
held in scorn. These vulgar poets, Graves writes,
were persistently transmitting their pre-Cymric tradition when certain Breton minstrels, travelling with
the Norman court, recognized and understood their
songs. The courtly bards, concerned with main-
taining their political interests, did everything they
could to discourage this revival.

The material "found" by the "trovères" was much
more virile than the complex stanzaic and metric
pieces favored by the bards—an aristocratic verse including the practices of *Cynghanedd* ("internal
rhyme") and *Dyfalu* ("image clusters") which were
to appear in the poetry of Hopkins and Dylan
Thomas. The pre-Cymric minstrels, meanwhile,
sang of the adventures of a warrior-king, his castle,
his death and voyage to the immortal island of *Yns
Avallach*. During this same early Norman period,
as Campbell points out in *Creative Mythology*, a
new poetry exalting the world of natural love as a
way to knowledge was permeating the *trovère* material from the east by way of Moorish Spain and
Provence. The synthesis of ancient Welsh, eastern-
erotic, and Norman-knightly strains was to emerge
as the tradition of a courtly King Arthur.

What can possibly be the significance of all of this to Dylan Thomas' prose and poetry? His early prose, as we shall see, is full of slippery and revolving islands occupied by woman or by a woman and her sisters, full of orchards containing female muses as well as inspirational apples, and full of island marshlands alternately flooding and drying—all used as settings for the heroes' quests for eros and, through eros, poetic inspiration. "Through my small, bonebound island I have learnt all I know, experienced all, and sensed all," wrote the young poet to Pamela Hansford Johnson in 1933. "All I write is inseparable from the island. As much as possible, therefore, I employ the scenery of the island to describe the scenery of my thoughts, the earthquake of the body to describe the earthquake of the heart."[8] In a slightly earlier letter he had described an actual island with which he had been uncomfortably identified from dusk to dawn one long night: he had gotten himself stranded on the "Worm," an islet off Rhossilli beach. A flat rock on the "Worm" he found "covered with long yellow grass," which made him feel "like something out of the Tales of Mystery and Imagination treading, for a terrible eternity, on the long hairs of rats."[9]

Here we have the personal metaphor, common enough in literature—"I am an island." But we also have a marked similarity to the landscape ascribed by Edward Davies to the pre-Cymric sites of worship. Davies describes islands, rather than oak-groves, as places of worship and burial.[10] One such location was Caer Sidi or Cader Idris (The Caer of the Sidhe?), supposedly Puffin Island off Anglesey, often described as a revolving tower or fairy castle. Geoffry of Monmouth, the first Norman chronicler to develop Arthur into a courtly knight, latinizes *Yns Avalach* or Isle of Avalon (mentioned in the sixth-century *Goddodin* of Aneurin and in Nennius' eighth-century *Historia Britonum*) as the *Insula Pomorum*, an island of fruit presided over by Morgan, the enchantress.[11]

Although it is as impossible as it is undesirable to separate the elements of a poetic symbology into personal and external sources, it would be a mistake to overlook the history of alternately flooding and drying lowlands around Swansea, the prehistoric caves upon the Gower Peninsula, and the grammar school accounts of local legend as influences upon the young poet. That he was somehow acquainted with the more recondite accounts of Welsh mythology popularized in the early nineteenth century by Davies is strongly suggested by analogies used both by Davies and by the poet. As I have pointed out in the Introduction, there is no evidence that either David John Thomas or his son ever heard of Davies' works. However, Dylan Thomas' tendency to combine symbols from biblical, Egyptian, and Welsh mythology can be compared to Davies' analogies between Noah, Osiris, and Dylan Ail Mor, while Thomas' mythological landscapes, female heroines, sun, and linguistic symbolism suggest an acquaintance with material more complex than the *Mabinogion.*

The amalgamation of earlier history into newer orthodoxies was a self-conscious procedure for which the Celtic druids trained their students, encouraging them to learn "not only the entire native mythological literature by heart but also the laws according to which mythological analogies were to be recognized and symbolic forms interpreted." This marriage of earlier, more secular myth to Christianity was pursued during the early Christian period both in "a reading of the symbolism of the Christian faith" and in "a recognition of analogies between this and the native pagan myths and legends."[12]

In the fifteenth century the historian Annius of Viterbo became interested in constructing a link between the patriarchal Hebrews and the Celtic race, a link which had fascinated the Irish clerics responsible for the syncretization of biblical and native materials found in the *Book of Kells*. In Wales, a similar tendency to fuse the transcendentally oriented Christian theology with an earlier, more immanent world view had produced the Pelagian heresy, far less delightful to mother church and persistent even into the nineteenth-century Unitarianism espoused by Great-Uncle William Thomas. Davies carried the syncretization of Celtic and Hebrew materials to its logical conclusion in a detailed parallelism between Noah and the pre-Cymric hero Dwyvach. Described by A. L. Owen as a "painstaking scholar" and by Robert Graves as "brilliant but hopelessly erratic," Davies developed a step-by-step analysis of the analogy between Celtic language and custom and the language and custom of the Hebrews and Egyptians. We are less concerned here with his tendencies toward mistranslation and anachronism than with his preoccupation with a primal, Edenic root-language (a preoccupation shared by the Brothers Grimm and the linguistic scholars in pursuit of Indo-European), the discovery of which would open God's own treasury of true poetry and song. His emphasis on language or "word" as organic, primal, and creative seems reflected in Dylan Thomas' narratives of floods, Noah-heroes, and quests for islands, orchards, and goddesses who hold the "first word," the source of inspiration, in their power. As we shall see, there are also striking similarities between the reputed druid processes of shaping analogies and Dylan Thomas' syncretization of Christian, mythological, and landscape materials.

III

I shall be concerned in this chapter with two main clusters of mythological figures: the one built around the flood-island-Noah-fertility theme, and the other around the figures of orchard, sun, language, and inspiration.

The flux and reflux of the sea tides have always been a matter of great concern to the inhabitants of the coast of Wales, where ocean floods invaded the land as recently as the sixteenth century. Raised beaches at Mewslade and submerged forests beneath Swansea Bay have provided material for both scientific and mythological speculation, as have the limestone caves with their prehistoric relics found

beneath Gower Peninsula. Wells running down
through the cliffs to the sea were natural formations
reputedly used by the ancient leaders to measure
the wind as well as the tide, for in stormy weather
they give off the mysterious wails of "blow holes."

Why east wind chills and south wind cools
Shall not be known til windwell dries
And west's no longer drowned
                                    (*CP*, p. 62)[13]

sings Thomas, who perhaps was looking forward,
as did his countrymen for centuries, to the restoration of the silver wood of Coed Arian drowned beneath Swansea Bay.

Thomas could have derived most of his knowledge of Welsh mythology from local legend. We
know, however, that he read the *Mabinogion* and
Peacock's *Misfortunes of Elphin*,[14] a parody of druid
theology which deals with the flood that destroyed
a small medieval kingdom. Edward Davies links
the chronic Welsh floods to a deluge which the
druids believed identical to the flood of the Biblical
Noah. This occurred as the first of "three awful
events of the Isle of Britain" and involved "the
bursting of the lake of waters, and the overwhelm-
ing of the face of all lands; so that all mankind were
drowned, excepting Dwyvan and Dwyvach, who es-
caped in a naked vessel (without sails) and of them
the island of Britain was re-peopled."[15]

Suzanne Roussilatt has suggested that Thomas'
extensive use of sea imagery in *18 Poems* (1934) and
Twenty-Five Poems (1936) sprang from his boy-

hood in a sea town.[16]   Actually, the entries in the earliest Poetry Notebooks contain little sea imagery, depending, rather, upon the vague inward surges of puberty with occasional excursions into parks and suburban fields for adornment. I would guess that before 1933, when the sea began its permanent invasion of his prose and poetry, Thomas had not become aware of the true significance of the one whose namesake he was. In September of 1933 he was still unaware of the meaning of his first name and wrote to Pamela Hansford Johnson that he thought it must mean "prince of darkness."[17] His fascination with the sea as a self-image and as a symbolic landscape begins in the poetry written at this time, however, and I would guess that sometime in the late thirties he learned that he had been named not for the devil but for the "son of the Wave."

From the *Mabinogion* alone he could have learned that Dylan was a golden, rascally fish-child of Arianrhod, who won for himself the name of Llew Llaw Gyffes (translated by Graves as "the Lion with the steady hand"). Arianrhod, writes Graves, "is one more aspect of Caridwen, or Cerridwen, the White Goddess of Life-in-Death and Death-in-Life" while Llew is "the usual handsome and accomplished Sun-hero with the usual Heavenly Twin at his side."[18] Although there is no evidence that Thomas was acquainted with the body of mythological material assimilated by Graves, it seems hardly accidental that he named his son Llewllyn (nicknamed "Llew") and his daughter Aeronwy. As we shall see in this chapter, moreover, the heroes of

Thomas' early tales seek to master both sun and sea in their quest for a feminine consort who is at one and the same time mother, sister, muse, and fate.

Dylan, Dy-Glaniaw ("to land or come ashore") or Dylan Ail Mor ("the son of the sea"), who was later celebrated as a heroic warrior born at St. Bueno's, appeared in early Welsh tradition as a god of both sun and sea. In the "helio-arkite rites" (which Davies repudiates but describes at length as a perversion of orthodox druidism) he is represented as a bull who pulls a sacred ark ashore. According to Joseph Campbell, bulls, buffalos, or mammoths are a constant in nearly every paleolithic mythology.[19] That they appear in the prehistoric worship of South Wales is evidenced by the mammoth tusks found around the "red lady" skeleton of the Gower caves.

Ploughing the land-kingdom of the earth goddess Kêd, the bull submits himself to a female deity of the land. "The billows of Dylan furiously attacked the shore," sings Casnodyn of another version of this landing.[20] In Thomas' "Ballad of the Long-legged Bait" the hero discovers that "the hills have footed the waves away," while the streets of

Rome and Sodom tomorrow and London
. . . .
. . . terribly lead him home alive
Lead her prodigal home to his terror
The furious ox-killing house of love.
(CP, p. 175)

In what may be a piece of early Romantic fantasy, Davies asserts that the central focus of druid worship was a "caer" or enclosed space meant to represent the original ark, located either on an island in the middle of an inland lake or on a hummock in the middle of a circular valley. "And where these were wanting," he concludes, "our hierophants seem to have constructed a kind of rafts or floats [*sic*] in imitation of such islands."[21] It is perfectly possible that Thomas became acquainted with such a landscape in Spenser's *Faerie Queene*, where there are many of

"those same Islands, which doe fleet
In the wide sea,"

courts where Phaedria and other earthy goddesses tempt the heroes to land. Whether he derived it from such a source or whether he invented it out of his head, the setting of an island in the midst of a lake or a hummock in the midst of an alternately flooding and drying valley plays an important part in many of his early tales.

Although William York Tindall has suggested that the title of "The Map of Love" (1934) might derive from Madelaine de Scudéry's seventeenth-century "Carte du Tendre," the landscape itself seems to be the dried out lake and sacred hill of druid mythology. "Beth Rib and Reuben marked the green sea around the island. It ran through the landcracks like a boy through his first caves. Under the sea they marked the channels, painted in skeleton, that linked the first beasts' island with the boggy lands" (*AST*, p. 146).[22] Here, while echoing his own boyhood quests upon Gower for skeleton caves, Thomas develops Beth Rib and Reuben as a primordial pair, prototypes of the innocent Adam and Eve. They travel through "the abominations of the swamp" left by a previous deluge in order to seek a "little island" that was once a sacred hill. On the sexual level this is the peak of coitus forbidden to childhood, an "adolescent hill" attained by the "white route of snow and ice" of fairy lore. On the mythological level it is the "heaven's hill" of Adam and Eve (see "I, in my intricate image," *CP*, p. 42 and "Incarnate devil," *CP*, p. 46) or possibly the Ararat of Dwyvan and Dwyvach. The island-hill of "the first beasts of love," it is surrounded by ancestral pastures where "Great-Uncle Jarvis," a Welsh patriarch, populates the nation with superhuman promiscuity. In order to reach the hill the children must pass through Jarvis' potent fields.

Although on the map the "first hill" is an island surrounded by sea, by the time of the children's journey it has become a mire of bog and mud. According to Davies, the pulling of an ark out of the swamp was accompanied by chants of encouragement to the yoked bulls and wails of horror at the "dark gore" which they trample.[23] In "The Enemies," "The Holy Six," and "The Visitor," the Jarvis valley groans and the grass is red with blood. In "The Map of Love" the country is alive with animal vitality: "For shame of the half-liquid plants sprouting from the bog, the pen drawn poisons seething in the grass, and the copulation in the second mud, the children blushed" (*AST*, p. 146). The sediments left by the deluge have become a land as corrupt as the antediluvian world: only by overcoming their fear of the corrupt vitality of the bog can the children redeem the natural cycle. The evil that they face is not so much the moral degeneration of the land as it is their inability to accept its erotic and literary ("pen drawn poisons") vitality. In their first attempt to pass through the bog and reach the hill, they are thwarted by their own tendency to repression.

In several of the early tales the action is divided into two parts or two journeys, a device similar to the double quest of grail legend and the two trials of folklore. This traditional narrative method enables Thomas to familiarize his reader with a complex symbolic landscape so that he can more easily grasp the significance of the final quest. In "The Map of Love" there is a third narrative level, that of the map itself. "Return, synthetic prodigals, to thy father's laboratory, declaimed Sam Rib, and the fatted calf in a test-tube." Sam, who is Beth's father and a Hardyesque master of fates, wields the controls of a scientific universe which relies upon human actors to carry out its processes. The abstract world of the map is a landscape of cartographic images, of cherubs representing "separate weathers" who mate as "two coupled countries" and "two naked towers." These map tokens resemble the imagery of a number of Thomas' early poems where towers, weathers, currents, and undersea sexual creatures appear over and over again. In the first section of "My world is pyramid" they take the form of underwater actors cloven into male and female "halves" which "swivel" around the sea. The children appear as such in "I, in my intricate image" where they climb "the country pinnacle" to meet "twelve winds . . . by the white hosts at pasture."

Only in "The Map of Love," however, is the quest of the child-couple described in a fully developed narrative context. They pass through the countryside of the map and of their first quest a second time to mount the sacred hill by swimming up the Idris River. Cader Idris, a mountain in Wales, had on its peak a stone seat where, according to legend, "whoever spends the night is found in the morning either dead, mad or a poet." Identified by Loomis with Puffin Island and by Davies as a typical island-sanctuary, Idris was also the first name of Dylan Thomas' cousin. His aunt Ann Jones, of Fern Hill, had a son Idris whom Thomas liked to describe "as a Welsh Heathcliff, perhaps a Carmarthenshire Billy Sunday, maybe a straight lunatic,"[24] and whom he immortalized as the hwylling (preaching) Gwilym of "The Peaches." It was probably in ironic honor of this cousin that Thomas gave his name to the children's river of erotic initiation.

In "The Map of Love" the children are concerned with the moon rather than with the sun, with carnal rather than with celestial knowledge. They plunge into the waters of sexual initiation in order to become a part of the mysteries of the origin of the race and the land which they live in. Their sexual union achieved, they bring about a "new moon" that floods the land. "Only the warm, mapped waters ran that night over the edges of the first beasts'

island," concludes Thomas. The waters suggest both
the amniotic or seminal fluids and the inland lakes
sacred to Welsh legend. The children's first intercourse is a wholly beneficial act, bringing about a
new deluge and a new cycle of generation.

"A Prospect of the Sea"—which deals with another
flood set in motion by sexual initiation ("The sea
had flowed and vanished, leaving a hill, a cornfield,
and a hidden house. . . .")—leads to a similar renewal of floods; the hero breaks out of childhood into
an inner world where Osiris and Isis, Noah and
Atlas, participate in his rite of manhood. At the
start of the tale the boy lies in his uncle's cornfield
telling himself stories of princesses, but the sight of
a real girl on a hill plunges him into levels of consciousness far deeper than fantasy. The two children exchange identities that are not Welsh but
Middle Eastern: he is "from Amman," and she has
a sister in Egypt who "lives in a pyramid." As she
draws him to her, the boy becomes terrified of both
the personal death of sexual initiation ("This is
death, said the boy to himself, consumption and
whooping-cough and the stones inside you. . . .")
and the impersonal death of the sun god who
drowns in the mother-sea ("his first terror of her
sprang up like a sun returning from the sea that
sank it. . . ." [*AST*, p. 127]).

As he makes love to the girl, he is no longer Osiris
but himself: "now he was a boy in a girl's arms, and
the hill stood above a true river, and the peaks and
their trees towards England were as Jarvis had
known them when he walked there with his lovers

and horses for half a century, a century ago" (*AST*, p. 127). Having established his hereditary link with Great-Uncle Jarvis through his own sexual initiation, the boy enters the world of mythological vision. He sees himself sailing "down the tide of the sun on to the grey and chanting shore where the birds from Noah's ark glide by with bushes in their mouths": from the biblical Ararat he marches "out of love" to the "last rail before pitch space." Voyaging eastward, he comes down beneath the earth to "the green Eden; and the garden was undrowned, to this next minute and forever, under Asia in the earth that rolled on to its music in the beginning evening." His sexual initiation has brought him back to the original place of human lovemaking, a return which renews both his own and the earth's vitality.

When the boy awakens he realizes that his lover is not mortal: she lives in the lands beneath the sea. She resembles the mermaid, common in Welsh folklore, who runs down into the sea to return to her people. On the personal or sexual level she represents his own latent femininity, on the mythological level an Isis-sister or Jungian *anima*. Thomas seems to link the Welsh floods that covered the forests of Arianrhod or the lands beneath Swansea Bay to the Biblical deluge, for as the boy runs after his lover he sees "an old man building a boat" while "the cloudy shapes of birds and beasts and insects drifted into the hewn door." In both "The Map of Love" and "A Prospect of the Sea," the Freudian pattern of wresting the lover-sister from the father (Sam Rib, Great-Uncle Jarvis) is suggested, as is the Jungian motif of

rebirth through a plunge into the waters of intercourse or into the depths of the unconscious. In both
cases, Thomas makes the children's achievement of
sexual intercourse set a new cycle of flood and regeneration in motion.

"A Prospect of the Sea" was followed by two fragmentary pieces which he was never to finish. In
these, "In the Direction of the Beginning" and "An
Adventure from a Work in Progress," the hero is more
like the "old man" of the earlier story than its boy-
hero: he sails on top of the sea in an ark-boat in quest
of an island-temptress who represents the sinister
type of female of the 1930-1932 Notebook and of such
poems as "Into her Lying Down Head," "Unluckily
for a Death," "Grief thief of time," and the "Ballad
of the Long-legged Bait." That these pieces were
important to Thomas, not merely discarded fragments, is suggested by the fact that he originally intended "In the Direction of the Beginning" as the title
piece of *The Map of Love* collection. "I have, however, been considering this piece," he noted in a February 1939 letter to David Higham, "and have now
decided to make it part of a much longer work which
I want to spread over many months to come."[25] This
larger work never came into being because of the
necessity to change to the more realistic prose style
of the later years in order to support his family.

In the first fragment the hero is an "Adam-man"
but born directly into corruption. He sets sail upon
a flood in his "shingled boat with a mast of cedar-
wood," a Noah's ark that is strangely "finned" and
sports "a salmon sail." According to Robert Graves,

Kêd was associated with the apocryphal Leviathan from which God created the earth[26] and, according to Davies, with the sacred ark which in the Welsh rites was represented by a coracle, a raft, or an island. In Thomas' two fragments, the Dylan-hero rides his fish-coracle to an island where, as in "Ballad of the Long-legged Bait," a land-goddess tries to destroy him.

The concluding part of the first fragment poses the riddle of "which was her genesis"—the beginning or end of the world. The woman now stands on the island luring and repelling the hero who wants to know whether she represents birth or death, creation or destruction. The answer, of course, is both: the word of creation and the last trump sound simultaneously over the island as "one voice . . . [that] travelled the light and water waves." "From the four map corners one cherub in an island shape puffed the clouds to the sea," concludes Thomas, with enigmatic simplicity. In "The Map of Love" cherubs served both as traditional map images of wind and as tokens that stand for the children: "The weathers, like a girl and a boy, moved through the tossing world, the sea storm dragging under them, the clouds divided in many rages of movement as they stared on the raw wall of the wind" (*AST*, pp. 146–147). In the *Rig Veda*, which Thomas acknowledged reading,[27] the weathers or Maruts occasionally "assumed again the form of newborn babes" to "toss the coulds across the surging sea."[28]

Far from minor deities in Indian mythology, the Maruts existed as the primordial forces of the universe before all other gods were born. In "A Prospect of the Sea" Thomas suggests his knowledge of these gods when he places the "weathers" above the "Heavens": the boy finds himself on "the world-sized hill, with the trees like heavens holding up the weathers." Where in "The Map of Love" and "A Prospect of the Sea" the cherub-weathers represent the force of innocent sexuality, in "In the Direction of the Beginning" and "An Adventure from a Work in Progress," they are subservient to a goddess of sensual perversion. This creature is not unlike the goddess of the *Rig Veda* who boasts, "On the world's summit I bring forth the father, my home is in the waters, in the ocean."[29] She may be related to the Celtic Banshee (Bean-She or White Woman), whom Graves describes as "the woman of the hill" wailing in prophetic anticipation whenever anyone of royal blood is about to die.[30] Her island recalls the silver or revolving island to which a number of sacred kings, including Arthur, sail at their deaths. In Thomas' two fragments she brings both death and rebirth: to embrace her is to lose one's identity in her ("He followed the flight of his name: it slipped to a stop at the peak; there a tall woman caught the flying name to her lips" [*AST*, p. 156]) and to be reborn ("Holding her small body, he cried in the nightmare of a naked child kissing and blaspheming close. . . ." [*AST*, p. 157]).

"An Adventure from a Work in Progress" is a continuation and a clarification of the first fragment. The hero sets out on two more quests for the island-woman, now on an "animal boat" symbolic of Noah's ark and perhaps of a higher stage of evolution than the fish-boat of "In the Direction of the Beginning." Like the fisher in the "Ballad of the Long-legged Bait" and the boy in "A Prospect of the Sea," he covers the globe from north to south. He seeks a "slowly spinning island" ringed with fire through which, like Siegfried, he must leap. Having achieved this first trial, he finds himself chasing the woman around the rim of the "roundabout island" but, like Rhianon in the *Mabinogion* tale of "Pwyll, Prince of Dyfed," she keeps the same distance from him.

The hero succeeds, nonetheless, and as he embraces the woman the island is suddenly "no longer spinning, but split into vanishing caves and contrary trees." The caves and trees, which on the sexual level represent the female and male organs, seem also to be mythological symbols of the sunken Eden and the tree of knowledge. Thomas' hero and heroine may be variations of the Noah and his wife who, according to Davies, appear in Welsh legend as Arthur and Gwenhwyvri—the "ark lord" and "the lady on the summit of the water." The spinning and splitting island—which appears also in "My world is pyramid," "A saint about to fall," "Poem on his Birthday," and "Author's Prologue"—seems to represent both the ovum split in gastrulation and the eternally dividing "Mundane Egg" of Blake's *Prophetic Books*.

At the denouement the woman becomes a mountain for the man to climb, but her "peak" is always just beyond him. The embrace which they finally achieve is destructive: the woman slides down the ladder of creation from girl to baby to monkey to fish to a white pool that spits in his hand. This degeneration resembles the fate of those who drink sabbatic wine in Machen's *The Great God Pan.* "I saw the form waver from sex to sex," declares Machen, " . . . then I saw the body descend to the beasts whence it ascended . . . I watched, and at last I saw nothing but a substance as jelly."[31] The embrace which the hero achieves brings him not only detumescence but also knowledge of life ("that the world might happen to him once") and of death. He participates in the Blakean fortunate fall from Edenic unity into "division and multiplicity," a condition necessary in Blake's writings to the eternal cycle of generation and regeneration.

IV

Whether or not Thomas' use of a landscape of alternately drying and flooding lands derives from a knowledge of local mythological material, each of the early prose tales is built upon a narrative line that is of mythological or fabulous nature. Kenneth Burke, discussing Caroline Spurgeon's application of a "*quantitative* test" (Burke's italics) to the number of images in a given work, asks whether there might not "also be the *qualitative* importance of beginning, middle, and end. . . . Hence, along with the distinction between opposing principles we should note the development *from what through what to what.*"[32] In both the poems and the prose of Thomas the development of the narrator or hero from incompletion to vision is often embodied in a struggle out of the sea, onto the land, and into the aegis of the sun.

In "When once the twilight locks no longer," Thomas describes both a journey into the sea and a struggle out of it. At the outset man is sent "scouting on the globe" by the creator, but quickly abandons the practice of "holding a little sabbath with the sun" to plunge into the damp world of instinct and sleep. The creator mourns that his creation has abandoned the bright world of consciousness for the undersea world of unconsciousness, but when he sends his "own ambassador to light" he does even worse, preferring a "carcass shape" of death to the world of light. In the last verse the creator calls upon the dormant Adam to awake "to the sun," leaving the "poppied pickthank" Christ behind in the world of dreams and death. The narrative line thus describes a progression out of the sea into the light, where the narrator must seek the "worlds" that "hang on the trees." "A process in the weather of the heart" describes a similar climb out of the tidal influence of the moon into the aegis of the "omnipotent sun," analogous to the journey of Marlais from the moon above the city to the apple orchards and their apotheosis of fire.

I have noted how, in the first section of "My world is pyramid," Thomas returns to the world of the underwater children. In the second section, however, Thomas announces an ascent onto the land: his world now "is pyramid," "cypress, and an English valley." The "fellow halves" become "tangled in the shells," and the androgynous child is buried secretly within the "half-tracked thigh." In the "Ballad of the Long-legged Bait" the hero finds his quest similarly entangled with land creatures as his ark is grounded and his sea bait transformed into his own "long-legged heart." In his late poem, "Author's Prologue," he takes on the character of a "Drinking Noah," setting out over the flooded Welsh lands where

Only the drowned deep bells
Of sheep and churches noise
Poor peace as the sun sets
And dark shoals every holy field.

(*CP*, p. xviii)

Like the hero of "In the Direction of the Beginning" and "An Adventure from a Work in Progress," Thomas begins his journey at the end of a cycle ("At God speed Summer's End"). In two tales central to Thomas' early prose both in the richness of their imagery and in the lyric beauty of their narrative delivery—"The Orchards" (1934–36) and "The Mouse and the Woman" (1932–1936)—the heroes journey to the seaside where they accept the governance not of the seawomen who beguile them but of the sun.

Dylan Ail Mor appears in later Welsh folklore as Merdin, Mer-Dain, or Merlin, the "comely one of the sea" to whom God gave the island of Britain as a gift. As he sailed toward England from the west to claim his gift, Merdin saw

Seven fair apple-trees, and seven score
Of equal age, height, length, and size;

One maid, with crisped locks guards them—
Olwedd is her name—of the form of *light* are her teeth.[33]

Apple orchards, sometimes enclosed like the arks in a quadrangular sanctuary and sometimes located on apple islands or Avalons, are reputedly sacred to the "rubicand, radiant Elphin," the British Apollo.[34]

Let the first Peter from a rainbow's quayrail
Ask the tall fish swept from the bible east
What rhubarb man peeled in her foam-blue channel
Has shown a flying garden round that sea-ghost?

declares Thomas in the last sonnet of "Altarwise by owl-light" (*CP*, p. 85), perhaps associating the fisher Merlin, ancient Peter, Leviathan, the woman of the sacred apple-island, and a rhubarb peddler.

According to Robert Graves, Olwedd is "the laughing Aphrodite of Welsh legend . . . Always connected with the wild-apple which is her symbol of the world and the sun."[35] In "The Orchards" and "The Mouse and the Woman" she appears as an orchard of seven trees; in "The Orchards" she is also a double female compounded of a "fair girl" and a "scarecrow." Its hero, who bears Thomas' middle name, Marlais (an anagram of Ail Mor?), is thus already a lord of the sea. He dreams of himself as an "apple farmer" with an orchard that is his heritage on the shores of Wales. He closely resembles the hero of *The Hill of Dreams* in his preoccupation with the occult ("The Women of LlanAsia") and the satanic ("The Black Book of Llaregubb"). Like Machen's hero he is unable to get anything onto paper but cold and esoteric imagery, and his story-women crumble before the reality of his own "hill of dreams" in the west of Wales.

After an unsuccessful attempt to mold his dream into art ("The morning was against him. He struggled with his words like a man with the sun, and the sun stood victoriously at high noon over the dead story" [*AST*, p. 98]) and a recurrence the next night of the dream ("Red sap in the trees bubbled from the cauldron roots to the last spray of blossom, and the boughs . . . fell like candles from the trunks but could not die for the heat of the sulphurous head of the grass burned yellow by the dead sun" [*AST*, p. 100]), Marlais finds that he must make an actual journey through the land of his ancestors. He walks first through industrial suburbs and then through the countryside in a return journey that might represent Thomas' own quest for his heritage in Swansea, Johnstown, and Carmarthen (or a typical walk from Swansea to Rhossilli on Gower). Once in the open country of his forebears, Marlais becomes "a folkman walking," taking on the archetypal identity of a Welsh hero upon a quest. Both Welsh epic heroism and the Christian heritage of heaven and hell must be passed by in this ritual journey as alien to an inward world where he must become "a folkman no longer, but Marlais the poet walking, over the brink into ruin. . . ." The journey takes place upon a high noon of midsummer, the time of summer fire sacrifices described by Frazer and of the midsummer Albans of the druids. Both correspond to Davies' second and third "awful events" of Welsh history, "the consternation of the tempestuous fire, when the Earth split asunder" and "the scorching summer, when the woods and plants were set on fire, by the intense heat of the sun."[36] In "The Orchards," "High noon, the story-killer and the fire bug . . . passed in all the high noons since the fall of man from the sun and the first sun's pinnacling of the half-made heavens" (*AST*, p. 101).

When he reaches the orchard by the sea, Marlais reenacts the movements of his dream: he greets the maiden, watches the apple trees catch fire, and kisses the "two secret sisters." "And he who had dreamed that a hundred orchards had broken into flame saw suddenly then in the windless afternoon tongues of fire shoot through the blossom. The trees all around them kindled and crackled in the sun, the birds flew up as a small red cloud grew from each branch, the bark caught like gorse, the unborn, blazing apples whirled down devoured in a flash" (*AST*, p. 103).

The consuming and regenerating sun of Marlais' orchard appears as a wholly destructive divinity in "The Mouse and the Woman." The hero, like Marlais, is a writer who dreams of trees, in this case a woman bewitched into a "black forest" of seven identical trees. The writer, no lover of the "harsh sun," dreams in a "lunatic blackness" alien to Marlais' fiery splendor. His consort is born, however, under the aegis of the sun, "one winter morning, after the last crowing of the cock." Having prided himself upon giving "being" to his nightmare by putting her "upon the block of paper," the hero walks down to the sea to find her awaiting him in the flesh.

Like the girl of "A Prospect of the Sea," the hero-

ine is an *anima* or feminine half who was one with
the hero "in the beginning" of the world and who
comes to life to be his consort. He goes through the
motions of Eden with her, walking in the garden and
achieving a first intercourse, but he is unable to accept her innocent sensuality or her "joy of created
life." Stumbling in the orchard in his dream, he
had felt "absurd in his nakedness"; now, telling the
girl that her nakedness is evil, he casts her out of
both his writing and his house. Alienated from the
source of his poetic inspiration and suddenly aware
of his mistake, he goes mad.

Thomas depicts the hero's state of mind by a
welter of garbled Egyptian and Freudian material.
The poet is haunted by his conscience, which appears to him as "an old effigy of time, his long beard
whitened by the Egyptian wind." This is probably
the demonic and Mosaic moralist who appears as
the villain Urizen in Blake's *Prophetic Books*.
Driven mad by an excess of reason and restraint, the
poet finds himself at war with "green Sirius, an eye
in the east," the dog star which in Egyptian astrology is associated with the hottest period of the year
and the time of the floods. Alienated from the god
of the sun, from his sevenfold orchard, and from the
renewing floods of the natural cycle, he is a mere
"parhelion" or false sun: "And all the elements come
together, of wind and sea and fire, of love and the
passing of love, closed in a circle around him" (*AST*,
p. 113). By breaking the rhythm of the seasons
within himself, he is forced to submit to the horrible
timelessness of the insane.

It might be argued that sea and sun, flood and fire are symbols available to any poet: why, in the case of Dylan Thomas, need a special point be made of derivation from Welsh, Egyptian, biblical, or any other mythological system? To those who feel that the basic level of the prose is sexual, are the landscapes not anatomically rather than archetypally derivative? That Thomas' lively countryside is an extension of the human anatomy is hardly to be denied: warm waters of birth, breasts of hills, phallic trees and caves are the setting for the heroes' quests for the peak of coitus in the embrace of their country girls. Were the sexual or Freudian level the only dimension of the tales, the elements of external mythological systems would have to be taken as extraneous and somewhat irrelevant decoration.

It is clear, however, that Thomas was creating tales of a specifically mythological nature. It seems likely that he had found Eugene Jolas' call for a mythological short story encouraging or at least compatible with what he had already achieved. In the July 1935 issue of *transition* Jolas conceived this new genre as "paramyth," a "successor to the form known heretofore as the short story or *nouvelle*." It would be "a kind of epic wonder tale giving an organic synthesis of the individual and universal unconscious, the dream, the daydream, the mystic vision. In its final form it might be a phantasmagoric mixture of the poem in prose, the popular tale of folklore, the psychograph, the essay, the myth, the saga, the humoresque."[37]

Thomas' heroes arrive at their mythological vision

through the initiatory gate of sexual intercourse, which gives them access to the inward world of human memory. Thus, in the process of becoming themselves, they become "folkmen," achieving with manhood a state of expanded consciousness where Noah, Osiris, Adam, and perhaps Dyglan are their "clayfellows," while Noah's wife, Isis, Eve, and perhaps Dwyvach are their bedfellows. The mysterious women who guard the gates of inspiration perform, in Thomas' highly individual setting, the function of the poetic muse.

The search for an eternally creative Word at the center of the universe is central to Thomas' narratives, whose heroes are, after all, his alter egos, questing over symbolic landscapes for a definitive, rich source of narrative and poetry. The quest to bind their vision back into a cosmic symmetry is religious in the root sense, and as such I will explore it in the following chapter.

CHAPTER III

Religion in the Early Prose

"God pronounced His Name, and with the word the world and its appurtenances, and all the universe leaped together into existence and life, with the triumph of a song of joy. The same song was the first poem that was ever heard, and the sound of the song travelled as far as God and His existence are."

Y Barddas

Critics differ sharply on Thomas' religion, or lack of it. Where W. S. Merwin finds him steeped in religious ritual, Stuart Holroyd declares that he gradually moved away from the "Christian attitude to life, which he could never find congenial, and became more confirmed in his pantheism."[1] Others argue that Thomas uses Christ as a metaphor for himself, heightening his personal drama through a mask of sacred archetype.[2] Through all this there is general agreement upon Thomas' debt to the chapel tradition. The 1930–1932 Notebook leaves little doubt that at one time he shared the Welsh chapel tendency to split the world into a Manichean division of heaven and hell. An emphasis on the Second Coming and its fulfillment of an apocalyptic cycle, which D. H. Lawrence found typical of Methodism in the midlands,[3] is also characteristic of

Thomas' writings. That he accepted the chapel insistence upon a personal confrontation with God is suggested by Christ's always personal and never doctrinal appearance in his poetry.

I

It has been assumed that the Bible and the chapel were the only religious influences upon Thomas' work. His poems and tales draw upon a wide range of mythological material, however; and even though it seems doubtful from what we are told of his scholarship and reading habits that he could have studied the volumes of Edward Davies, we have seen how Davies' account of "Welsh mythology" casts some light upon the structure and detail of the key prose tales. Similarly, although it is generally held that Williams ab Ithel's *Y Barddas* was a hoax, his systematization of purportedly bardo-druidic beliefs into a coherent solar religion is of relevance to Thomas' symbology.

This collection of catechetical dialogues was the sole entry in an 1858 eisteddfod, a revival of the old bardic gatherings of the poets. A prize had been offered for the best compilation of materials concerning the "Bardo-druidic system of the Isle of Britain,"[4] and ab Ithel, rising to the bait, produced the works of Iolo Morganwyg, whom he claimed was an eighteenth-century scholar and heir to the main line of bards. Morganwyg, Graves notes, was celebrated as an "improver of Welsh documents" rather than as a bard: it was from his library, nonetheless, that Lady Guest's version of the *Mabinogion* was drawn.

We know from Caesar's account that the druids were as much concerned with astronomy as with poetry; one may speculate that in the early Christian centuries there might have been some influence upon the druids from the Mithraic cult of Sol Invictus, instituted as the imperial religion by Aurelian (ruled A.D. 270–275) and carried into the provinces by Roman soldiers.

Sun gods, Sons of God, Words of Light and the Logos are familiar in contemporary Christianity: "He is risen!" shout twentieth-century devotees as the sun appears over the horizon early on Easter morning. Are they celebrating the rebirth of a deity named Christ or of one named Sol who shares his birth date, December 25? The association of the Christian God with the God of the Sun is only a recent instance in an historic series of assimilations: "Since syncretization was no less congenial to the native religions of Europe than to those of the Orient," remarks Campbell, "there developed throughout the Post-Alexandrian world—from Scotland to North Africa and Eastward into India—. . . a single, rich and colorful religious empire with an infinite wealth of forms, joining and harmonizing on many levels all the pantheons of the nations: Celtic, Germanic, Roman, Greek, and Oriental."[5] Apparently taking part in the same nineteenth-century quest for a "root language" and historical, organic religion as Davies, ab Ithel insisted that Morganwyg's *Y Barddas* was the basic work in ethics, theology, and natural science that had to be memorized by each bardic aspirant. What he presents is, of course, a system of solar religion, practices, and poetics assimilated with Welsh history, folk belief, the occult, and Christianity.

According to ab Ithel's compilation bardic theology was so assimilative that it easily absorbed medieval Christianity. "There are three special doctrines that have been obtained by the nation of the Cymry," declares one contributor to the Y Barddas collection: "the first, from the age of ages, was that of the Gwyddoniaid [patriarchal sages] prior to the time of Prydian [1216–566 B.C., Welsh chronology] . . . ; the second was Bardism, as taught by the Bards, after they had been instituted; the third was Faith in Christ, being the BEST OF THE THREE."⁶ The earliest doctrine was shared with the druids in Gaul and western Europe; the second is the uniquely Welsh system instituted to preserve this doctrine against assimilation. The Christian revelation was considered the logical fulfillment of the earlier traditions.

We learn from Y Barddas that the druid patriarchs taught that the universe was divided into three concentric spheres. In Y Barddas the white space of Ceugant was described as the innermost circle, at the center of which the sun was revered as the symbol or representative of God. Around Ceugant spun the circle of Gwynvyd, occupied by those men who had attained vision and knowledge. The outermost sphere contained the earth and all living things. It was named *Abred*, or "the circle of courses" from one form of material existence to another. At the edge of Abred, at the very circumference of the universe, lay *Annwyn*, a region of outer darkness where life came as close as possible to ultimate death.

This universe had sprung into being when God sent forth the *Logos* in the form of three rays. "Co-instantaneously with the voice was light, and in the light, form," declares *Y Barddas*[7] and in the song of joy at the earth's beginning all knowledge, poetry, and music had their origin. From the three rods of the Logos were formed the first ten letters of the Welsh alphabet. These and the craft of writing were taught to each bardic initiate, but the original triad or *awgrym* (symbol) remained an unspeakable and probably lost secret.

"I have desired the circle of the sun," declares Thomas,[8] who may have had a Welsh as well as a Christian perspective on Genesis. In his world's beginning "was the three-pointed star" and "the word / That from the solid bases of the light / Abstracted all the letters of the void" (*C.P.*, p. 27).[9] The three elements of light, sound, and shape appear in many of his references to the Logos. At the denouement of "In the Direction of the Beginning" the new cycle is heralded by "one voice" which "travelled the light and water waves"; and in "From love's first fever to her plague" Thomas declares that the four winds "Shone in my ears the light of sound, / Called in my eyes the sound of light" (*CP*, p. 24). When in "Prologue to an Adventure" the hero remembers "the golden sexless men that cried All Praise in the sounds of shape," Thomas goes on to explain that "we are all metaphors of the sound of shape of the shape of sound, break us we take another shape." A poem, like a man, is a molding of sound, shape, and light: in "The Visitor" when Peter tried to make a last poem he "rounded a little ball of sound into some shape, and spoke a word."

According to Graves and Davies the letters of the Welsh alphabet were originally symbolic: *Beth* or B, for example, representing the concept of being. Later, probably under religious persecution, each letter was given a code-tree—*Ailm* (fir) for A, *Birch* for B, and so on. From a combination of branches and leaves of these special trees the bards built up a system for communicating upon philosophical and practical matters. One such tree-statement could be taken as a précis of "The Orchards"; "The point of the apple tree, supporting blossoms, proud covering of the wood, declares—everyone's desire tends to the place of his affections."[10] "Calligraphy of the old / Leaves is dancing," declares Thomas in "A Winter's Tale," and in "Especially when the October wind" he offers to tell the reader the secret "of the vowelled beeches" and the "oaken voices." In Thomas' prose and poetry the frequent appearance of a "tree of words," or "book of trees" suggests a combination of the biblical tree of good and evil and the bardic tree of knowledge. (See "Altarwise by owl-light," Sonnets IV and VII, *CP*, pp. 81–83.)

II

The druids considered man a union of opposite natures, a conjunction of dead matter and spirit that inspired them with a deep awe of creation and an equally deep horror of bodily degeneration. Utter death, *Cythraul*, occurred only once, at the beginning of the universe before matter was stirred into being. At that time God, "uniting Himself with the lifeless, that is, the evil, with the intention of subduing it unto life, imparted the existence of vitality to animated and living beings, and thus did life lay hold of the dead."[11] Although no one ever enters the outer darkness beyond Annwyn, before birth and after death each person must journey to the lowest forms of life and proceed from there to his next incarnation. The bards, endowed with the ability to remember their previous transmigrations, sang of their descent into Annwyn in their works.[12] After the advent of Christianity in Wales they upheld Christ as a supreme example of one whose spirit dwelt in flesh and who journeyed into Annwyn for the sake of fuller incarnation.

"I, born of flesh and ghost, was neither a ghost nor man, but mortal ghost," declares Thomas' Christ (*CP*, p. 9). In "I dreamed my genesis" he could be describing a dream-journey into the lowest circle of the universe:

A creature in my bones I
Rounded my globe of heritage, journey
In bottom gear through night-geared man.
                    (*CP*, p. 33)

Certainly in "The Visitor," (1954) one of his finest prose tales, Thomas treats the death of the poet Peter in a peculiarly bardic manner. Near the beginning he announces that "a man with a brush had drawn a rib of colour under the sun and painted many circles around the circle of the sun."[13] At the conclusion of the tale he describes the same painter drawing a red rib "down the east," perhaps representing Peter's journey back to the beginning of things across the circle of material existence.

The druids of Y *Barddas* taught that at death the body returns as near as possible to the original four elements—*Calis* (corporeality), fluidity, breath, and fire—and that the soul proceeds through this dread experience to its next incarnation. In "The Visitor," death visits Peter as Callaghan (*Calis*-man?) and takes him to a valley where the process of return to the elements is in motion. Peter's agon falls into two movements: a daydream of life and the sun, and a nightdream of the moon and death. In the first movement Peter lies on his bed, loathing the clockwork objectification of his dying body. The same conflict of object and subject or matter and spirit underlies the difficult "All all and all the dry worlds lever" and "I, in my intricate image." He is tended by Rhianon, a spirit of the sunlit clover-and-milk world who does battle with Callaghan, spirit of dryness, darkness, and death: "Callaghan was the west wind, and Rhianon blew away the chills of the west wind like a wind from Tahiti" (*AST*, p. 78). In Y *Barddas* Rhianon appears as a muse whose birds "sang until the Angels of Heaven came to listen to them," a sister to the goddess Awen who sprang from the Logos to preside over poetry and learning.[14] Thomas' "West death," feared also by the children of "The Map of Love," is the death of the setting sun, and he was probably also aware of a traditional location of Annwyn to the west of Wales.

After musing about his past and his work, Peter drifts into a daydream governed by the sun. He feels his body turn into an island "set somewhere in the south caverns," a summer country overgrown "with the rich and miraculous plants." Beneath the cool waters on which his island floats grows an olive tree, a "tree of words." Peter awakens, tries to drink water, and is lulled back to sleep by Rhianon's reading of a passage from *The Book of Thel*. Blake's poem is an appropriate introduction to the second movement: it concerns a virgin-spirit who does not want to become mortal because of her fear of death-in-life.

In *Y Barddas* there are three kinds of light—of the sun, of alchemy, and of the soul—and in "The Visitor" Callaghan blows out Peter's three candles of life over his protests that there must be "light, light, light." Together they run naked to a "green globe of soil," a hummock above the Jarvis valley. Death has invaded the dry valley in a deluge of blood:

From their holes in the flanks of the hills came the rats and weasels, hairs white in the moon, breeding and struggling as they rushed downward to set their teeth in the cattle's throats. No sooner did the cattle fall sucked on to the earth and the weasels race away, than all the flies, rising from the dung of the fields, came up like a fog and settled on the sides. . . . Now the sheep fell and the flies were at them. . . . It was to Peter but a little time before the dead, picked to the symmetrical bone, were huddled in under the soil by the wind that blew louder and harder as the fat flies dropped on to the grass. (*AST*, p. 83)

Callaghan's Jarvis valley is an apocalyptic country where a cycle of destruction and regeneration is in full motion. It is a variation on the fields full of "second mud" in "The Map of Love" and the bogs of Egyptian relics in "An Adventure from a Work in Progress."

From his hill Peter sees the carnage terminate in a sea of blood which "flowed over the ground, strengthening the blades of the grass, fulfilling the wind-planted seeds in its course, into the mouth of the spring." Like Yeats' Lapis Lazuli Chinamen, Peter laughs gaily at the ongoing life. Callaghan returns his laugh mockingly, amazed that he should find "life in this nakedness," and at his cynical laugh Peter's heart bursts with disappointment. At this "a life burst out of the pebbles" and "the streams again went on their way . . .": Peter's death in disappointed affirmation of life renews the coursing of the material cycle.

To the critic concerned with Thomas' religion, the question raised by "The Visitor" is whether he is describing a pantheistic vision of natural death. For the pantheist all things are organic, neither the individual soul nor the divinity is transcendent, and man achieves dignity through his chemical union with the natural world. Peter's dream of death is certainly pantheistic: he glories in the return of life to its simplest elements. The tale does not end with his physical death, however: like the bards, Peter seems to descend into Annwyn in full possession of his conscious faculties, and like them he returns. The story concludes as he awakens, fully aware of his identity as Peter the poet, to find Rhianon pulling the sheet over his dead face. Thomas rejects the strictly pantheistic denouement for one which affirms the tragic fusion of matter and consciousness that is the human individual.

Although they play an important part in the structure of "The Visitor," the bardo-druidic cosmography and theory of the process of death appear chiefly as symbolic detail in the poems and prose. The bardic search for the Logos, for the maiden who guards it or for the tree which bears its derivations, seems more fundamental to the prose tales. In Welsh theology there seems to be no original "fall," since everyone but God is excluded from the white circle of Ceugant; the Welsh search for Genesis is not so much a quest for innocence as for the source of verbal life. This quest is implicit in "In the Direction of the Beginning," "An Adventure from a Work in Progress," "A Prospect of the Sea," "The Map of Love," and "The Mouse and the Woman," but it is in the definitive and complex "The Orchards" that it receives its fullest treatment.

The original version of "The Orchards" was entitled "Anagram," perhaps a variation on the bardic "awgrym." Mr. Tritas, the hero, seeks a word writ-

ten in the moon above the city. In the much length-
ier final version Marlais' journey is not only an archetypal "folkwalk," as we have seen in Chapter 2, but
also a semantic journey through types of word and
image to the sources of language.

At the start Marlais is a mere "image of man,"
tormented by his more substantial identity as "man-
in-a-dream-Marlais." In order to rid himself of his
philological virginity he "moves for the last answer"
through lands of extraneous verbiage where guides
provide epithets for his goal ("the wine-coloured
sea," "the mermaid-crowded sea"). He must avoid
"Aberbabel's chapel" of verbal confusion and pass
beyond the Protestant doctrines spoken by the "red
hot voices" of hell. He seeks a place where Welsh
and Christian theology have assimilated, where
"new trees arise, making an orchard round the
crucifix."

The quest takes place over a landscape that seems
to be derived from druid cosmography: it is a "turning world" with the "circle of the town" whirling at
the circumference in a confusion of cars, streets,
dust, marzipan, and babies. Marlais walks through
the "circles that travelled over the shady miles" until
he comes to the "apple circles" at the "green centre"
of his world. There on a hill near the sea Marlais
sees spirit and matter, apple and fire meet, consume,
and blossom at one and the same time. Where the
children in "The Map of Love" and "A Prospect of
the Sea" were concerned with initiation into the
natural cycle, Marlais and Peter seek an explanation
for its periodic rupture by death. "This was the end

of a story more terrible," declares Thomas of "The Orchards," "than the stories of the quick and the undead in mountainous houses on Jarvis hills ["The Enemies," "The Holy Six," "The Horse's Ha," "The School for Witches"] and the unnatural valley that Idris waters ["The Map of Love"] is a children's territory to this eleventh valley in the seaward travel" (*AST*, p. 104). Peter hovering above his own body, comprehending its death, and Marlais raised above the natural cycle by vision both achieve a state similar to Gwynvyd, the enlightenment of the bards.

III

In *Y Barddas* Christ is the third, last, and best "restoration" of the ancient teachings, a dweller and a "Name of God" in Abred. Having achieved the state of Gwynvyd he guides the dead on their journeys through Annwyn to new life. An example of the greatest possibilities of mortality, he had come like the bards "through every form capable of a body and life, to the state of man along the circle of Abred . . ." and was experienced "in every incident, in every suffering" of human life.[15] Since no one but the divinity may dwell in Ceugant, he is not "one with God" in the orthodox sense. He is, rather, a hero whose complete experience of material and human existence is to be admired and emulated. Like Blake's "fourth Zoa," his incarnation in the inner world of an individual and his alliance with the poetic imagination unite the warring faculties of the individual.

In Thomas' poetry Christ goes through all the forms of life from the bardic "lowest water amiculae"—as in "Before I knocked"—to the death on the cross. Like Noah and Adam he is the poet's "clay-fellow," wed to him through their common manhood. The poet's birth is his birth, he is his familiar "Jack Christ," and his cross becomes the poet's "nest of mercies in the rude, red tree." Although Christ does not appear in person in any of the early tales, there are elements of Christian ritual admixed with Welsh, occult, and personal materials in almost every one.

If god is praised in poem one
Show no surprise when in the next
I worship wood or sun or none:
I'm hundred-heavened and countless sexed

declares Thomas in a marginal scribble in the August 1933 Notebook.[16] His religion, like that of the bards, is assimilative. In "The Orchards," the crucifix is absorbed into a Welsh orchard Golgotha, and in "The Visitor" Christ is a metaphor for Peter: when Rhianon washes him he muses that "Such a woman had washed the body after it had been taken off the tree. . . ."

There are few Christian references in the stories which deal chiefly with sexual initiation—those that there are I have considered in Chapter 2. In several tales which I shall study in the following chapter, Christian rites are married to occult and sabbatic practices. There are two instances, however, in which Thomas achieves a unique synthesis of Christianity and personal material: "The Tree" and the unpublished "Gaspar, Melchior, Balthasar."

The hero of "The Tree" is a child whose experience is more primitive than that of the children in "The Map of Love" and "A Prospect of the Sea." Like them, however, he has a head full of stories and an imagination that insists upon bringing them to life. He lives alone in a house in a green valley surrounded by the Jarvis hills, where no one comes except a gardener and an idiot. The gardener is his "Sam Rib," who instructs him about the landscape and its significance. Central to the valley is the elder tree in the midst of the garden which the gardener reveres as a type of the tree of Calvary and Eden. "Always pray to a tree . . . ," he tells his charge, for God grows up like a tree "from the apple-shaped earth." This combination of Welsh and Christian legend leads the boy into an animistic worship of the tree for its own sake.

In the Welsh tree alphabet the elder, *Ruis,* was associated with witches. It represented the thirteenth letter and was considered extremely unlucky, a "tree of doom." Whether or not Thomas was aware of these legendary attributes, the elder in "The Tree" has exactly this sinister significance. Near it stands a tower which the boy is not allowed to enter. On Christmas the gardener, having no gift, unlocks the tower instead. The boy explores it but is wildly disappointed that there are no secrets except for the view of the Jarvis hills from the high window. Remembering that the gardener had told him that Christ came from the east and that the Jarvis hills lay eastward, he is calmed by the thought that he now knows the location of Jerusalem.[17] The next morning, when he finds an idiot from across the hills standing under the elder, he is convinced that he has found Christ himself.

The idiot had stood the evening before on the edge of the valley, "hungry for light as the first and almost invisible rain fell on his lips. . . ." Sipping at the rain, he communed with the created world until "there was light in his mouth, and light was a sound at his ears, and the whole dominion of light in the valley that had such a curious name" (*AST*, p. 74). Like the boy he is so close to nature that he "brothers" it in a manner that seems as much bardic as animistic: "The life of the Jarvis valley, streaming up from the body of the grass and the trees and the long hand of the stream, lent him a new blood." Like Peter and the Welsh Christ he is given life by participation in the cycle of the natural world. On Christmas morning the little boy, remembering the "Calvary and Eden" of the gardener's story, crucifies the idiot upon the elder.

In an earlier version of the story Thomas couched the narrative in slightly gentler terms, describing the love that the dead mother bore for the child. In this version,[18] where he is searching for his mother, the killing of the idiot bears some relation to his grief and guilt at her death. In the final version all references to the mother are deleted so that the story stands upon the relation of the child to gardener, tower, and tree. The result is a stark ritual killing through which the boy initiates himself into the only reality he knows. For Thomas each person must partake of the birth and death of Christ if Christianity is to be real. The child in "The Tree," in his primitive manner, is following the quest of Peter, Marlais, and the bards through dream and story to the realization of his own portion of psychic mystery.

"I was in the place of the crucifixion of the merciful son of God!" declares Taliesin,[19] to whom participation in Christ's life was as essential as Christ's participation in his. Similarly, in Thomas' work Christ is born with the descriptions of birth in such early poems as "Before I knocked," "If I were tickled by the rub of love," and "Do you not father me." In "Gaspar, Melchior, Balthasar" he emerges from the virgin's womb into the rubble of modern war. The piece is similar in its theme of birth in death to "Ceremony after a Fire Raid" (1944), save that in the tale the child is born out of rather than destroyed within the air raid. In the story Thomas walks in the person of the narrator through an urban Jarvis valley, a city under bombardment. The streets are acrawl with death, filled with reeking corpses and black flowers blossoming from them. Where in "The Visitor" Peter surveyed the Jarvis valley "in his ghost" or spiritual intellect, here two "ghosts" walk the streets in search of some living thing.

Following these spirits, Thomas comes upon a freshly bayonetted woman in the midst of the machine gunfire and corpses. The three watch a child struggle out of the wound in her belly. The two ghosts bow down in worship, one offering gold and the other frankincense. Thomas suddenly finds himself on his knees offering myrrh, and at that moment he is shot through the heart. A victim of modern war, he becomes the "black king," the third and deathly participant in a ritual of epiphany.

The most compelling evidence that Thomas might have known bardic theology is the uniqueness of his Christ. It is impossible to believe either that as the sperm in "Before I knocked" he is merely a sexual symbol or that as the brilliantly hymned figure of "Vision and Prayer" he is a mere stage mask lending drama to the poet's ego. It is in this poem, a lyric masterpiece, that Thomas' religious attitude towards the figure of incarnate Christ is most fully realized.

At the beginning of the world of "Vision and Prayer" there is a "first death," "The woundward flight of the ancient / Young from the canyons of oblivion!" (CP, p. 159). After this one experience of ultimate nihilism there is, as in "A Refusal to Mourn," "no other" final dying for the human soul, even though each man must return over and over to "the round / Zion of the water bead" (CP, p. 112). For this, much more than for the reasons given by the pantheist, "death shall have no dominion." Every aspect of Thomas' peculiarly Welsh Christ is on fire in "Vision and Prayer": the poet is lost "In / The spin / Of the sun," caught "In the caldron / Of his / Kiss," and blinded by the "High noon / Of his wound." Although Thomas, like Peter, prays for the "known dark" where the "country of death is the heart's size," he and his works are caught up in an apotheosis of "crimson / Sun."

The same violent entry of divinity into matter

that haunts Thomas as it did Hopkins seems also to underlie "In country sleep," where Christ may well be the "Thief" hailed by a "sermon / Of blood" and "the gospel rooks." "Vision and Prayer" concludes with what seems a triumph of the Welsh solar divinity, roaring and blinding "at the prayer's end."

CHAPTER IV

Blake and the Occult
in the Early Prose

*"By an apocalypse I mean primarily the imaginative conception of
the whole of nature as the content of an infinite and eternal living
body which, if not human, is closer to being human than to being
inanimate."*

Northrop Frye, Anatomy of Criticism

The religious and poetic quest for the Logos that
characterizes the work of Yeats, T. S. Eliot, James
Joyce, Dylan Thomas, and a number of their contemporaries runs parallel to the occult search for a
life-creating primordial Word at the center of the
universe. Whether dignified by scholarship (as in
the case of Plotinus, Giordino Bruno, Böhme, and
others) or pursued underground in forbidden cults
(as in the case of the alchemists, Hermetics, Kab-
balists and Rosicrucians), the same divinity is
sought: one who will not remain unapproachably
"other" but who can be encircled by rituals and embodied in verbal incantations. Bruno might burn
but the tradition continues: "The High God," explains Charles Williams, "had submitted himself to
formulae. He sent his graces, He came Himself,
according to ritual movements and ritual formulae.
Words controlled the God."[1]

The desire to naturalize the transcendent God was, as we have seen in previous chapters, endemic to Ireland and Wales; but British scholarship is hardly immune. The seventeenth-century Hebraists Robert Fludd and Thomas Vaughn claimed "to provide an account of the relationship between Man and God and Nature in its permanent, historic character. From the Hebraic point of view, Jerusalem is not a mythical ideal but rather one capable of resurrection in history through the exercise of our human faculties."[2] This resurrection was to be effected exactly in the manner of Edward Davies' later Welsh researches, by a syncretization of Old Testament and pagan materials. The law of nature was to be conceived in Hebraic or "Noahidic" rather than pagan terms.

I

"And was Jerusalem builded here / Among these dark Satanic Mills?" asked Blake, carrying on in his own unique manner the historic and syncretistic tradition. Having read Böhme and converted to the occult church of Swedenborg, Blake followed in a more individualistic and heady manner the early tradition of Henry More, Cudworth, and Sir Thomas Browne. Where they had desired a harmony between the Book of Genesis and the Platonic worldview, he carried the quest undaunted into an amalgamation of the New Testament and contemporary (in this case, late Augustan) England, singing of the revitalized individual psyche and social body as a "New Jerusalem." Explicitly vitalistic in *The Marriage of Heaven and Hell* (written during the first flush of enthusiasm over the French Revolution, in 1789–1790), Blake was his own man, diverging both from Swedenborg and—like the Cambridge Platonists—from advocates of a "mechanistic" or "natural" religion. Like Dylan Thomas, who followed directly in his sexual and religious enthusiasms, Blake constructed his work upon the dialectic of nature and imagination, between the natural and the supernatural.

Blake's younger contemporaries, Wordsworth and Coleridge, were no less immune to the fascinations of neo-Paganism: both attended the Cambridge of Paley. Coleridge, as Abrams points out, based his plant-poetry analogies upon the "aesthetics of organicism" which he absorbed both at Cambridge and in Germany.[3] Wordsworth spent his entire poetic life wrestling between the love of nature ("Great God! I'd rather be / A pagan suckled on a creed outworn") and conformity to orthodox Christianity. ("Our souls have sight of that immortal sea / Which brought us hither"). The second generation of Romantics was to carry the new Renaissance to its peak—in Shelley's humanistic epics, Byron's Satanism, and Keats' rich, areligious lushness one can sense the persistent tradition of pagan naturalism.

During the Victorian period, with Tennyson's doubts and Arnold's despair pouring forth from the historical and religious wounds dealt by Darwin, the occult traditions in England simmered only a few inches underground. These were the great years of Madame Blavatsky, whose *Isis Unveiled* and

Secret Doctrine introduced Theosophy, a "synthetic religion," as William York Tindall describes it, "that, embracing the Oriental and the occult, is good for those who are weary of Huxley and Tyndall."[4] In Wales, as we have seen, atheism—as well as the liberal Unitarianism espoused by Great-Uncle William Thomas—became widespread in the late nineteenth century: Dylan Thomas, like Yeats, belongs to a second generation of free thinkers perhaps "weary" of vapid Unitarian reasonableness.

II

In the occult traditions the divinity submits himself to charts and diagrams as well as to ritual and verbal formulae. His body, marked with its ten virtues, elements, or "emanations" is as "The Sacred Tree of the Sephiroth" the central object of Kabbalistic reverence. His omnipotence springs from his androgynous inclusion of male and female: the mother, father, "bride" and ten female emanations are absorbed into his personality so that he has the glory of Adam before the creation of Eve and of the biblical Word "at the right hand of God" before the creation of the world. In the fallen world, however, his Shekinah or Eve-bride is divided from him, and only if she returns can he regain his primordial strength: "the complete integration in her of all the branches of the Sephirotic Tree will not take place til he comes Who shall be called Man, that is Adam or SHILOH."[5]

When, in an unpublished poem, "Shiloh's seed," Thomas announces that

Through the floodgates of the sky
Grains of seed shall be dropped loose,
Manna for the hungry globe,
Quickening for the land and sea,[6]

it seems more likely that he had in mind the occult world-divinity than the biblical land of Shiloh. "Thomas' own footnote," writes Maud in a note to the poem, "refers us to Johanna Southcott (1750–1814), a domestic servant who identified herself with the 'woman clothed with the sun' of Revelation. Although sixty-four she promised to give birth to a son, the Shiloh of Genesis 49:10."[7] Even if he had perused some edition of the *Kabbalah*[8]—the "twenty fields" of "The Map of Love" and "The Holy Six" with the phallic "tenth and central field" could refer to the Kabbalistic number symbolism— he was probably more profoundly influenced by Blake's *Prophetic Books*.

The "myth of a primeval giant whose fall was the creation of the present universe is not in the Bible itself," notes Frye, "but has been preserved by the Cabbala in its conception of Adam Kadmon, the universal man who contained within his limbs all heaven and earth, to whom Blake refers."[9] At the start of Blake's *The Four Zoas, Milton,* and *Jerusalem* a worldman is divided off from his consort as the earth falls from eternity into time. This division of a primordial androgynous divinity occurs through an excess of reason which also brings about the repression and rebellion of the emotions. The hero's mind is split in two from the tension between eighteenth-century "natural philosophy" and the demands of romantic imagination, between "common sense" and sexual desire. The consort departs, lamenting the "Laws of Chastity and Abhorrence" imposed upon her, while the other emanations turn to the comfort of stringent piety or moralism. The hero's unconscious desires are chained down only to rage in repression: he passes into a coma where the rest of the action takes place between his warring faculties—Urizen (You Reason) Luvah (Lover, desire), and Los (Sol, the sun, the creative imagination).

In Blake's system the regeneration of the individual cannot take place until Satan, the once angelic being now Lord of the inner world, is reconciled to reason and consciousness. The whole of "Milton" is devoted to Milton's reconciliation with the Satan whom, according to Blake, he had unwarrantably maligned in *Paradise Lost*. The apocalyptic reunion of the human faculties, of man and woman, and of the universe with God is preceded, in each Prophetic Book, by the arrival of Satan or of an Antichrist. "Without contraries is no progression. Attraction and Repulsion, Reason and Energy, Love and Hate are necessary to human existence."[10] The apocalyptic scenes at the end of each prophetic book regenerate creation in a manner similar to the dark dance in Thomas' Jarvis valley:

Timbrels and violins sport around the Wine-presses; the little Seed,
The sportive Root, the Earth-worm, the gold Beetle, the wise Emmet,

Dance around the Wine-presses of Luvah: the Centi-
      pede is there,
The ground Spider with many eyes, the Mole clothed in
      velvet

. . . .

They throw off their gorgeous raiment: they rejoice with
      loud jubilee
Around the Wine-presses of Luvah, naked & drunk with
      wine

No more than Peter of "The Visitor" are the human
beings allowed to glory "in the swinish plains of
carrion":

But in the Wine-presses the Human grapes sing not nor
      dance
But howl and writhe in shoals of torment, in fierce
      flames consuming.[11]

Because of his greater endowment both of imagination and consciousness man suffers in the regeneration of the earth: the poet Los must be purged and
united with the crucified Christ, the fourth Zoa, before he triumphs as the governing human faculty.

   "I believe that Blake was not emphasizing the sexual act entirely for its own sake," writes S. Foster
Damon. "I think he found that it induced the
proper mental state in which to write poetry or to
imagine pictures."[12]   In Thomas' tales the hero's
sexual initiation is often related to his taking on of
a mythological identity.   He seeks out a consort who
has the characteristics of an "emanation" rather than
of a distinct individual: in "A Prospect of the Sea"
the boy becomes Osiris in the embrace of Isis, in

"The Map of Love" the children are described as a "double-climber" seeking the "first beasts' island," while in "The Mouse and the Woman" the hero "at last gave birth to her who had been with him from the beginning." "Man was the burning England she was sleep-walking," declares Thomas of the heroine of "Into her Lying Down Head," and Blake's sleeping Albion may well be lying in "the androgynous dark" beneath a number of his works.

III

Thomas' early prose tales are constructed upon a thematic conflict of innocence and experience, waking and sleeping, quest and renewal, which seems less an absolute progression from one state to another than a moment in an eternally wheeling cycle of contrary forces. In *Apocalypse* D. H. Lawrence compares the Christianity of Revelation popular in Welsh and midland Methodism to the pagan "method of the Apocalypse" which tended "to set forth the image, make a world, and then suddenly depart from this world in a cycle of time and movement and event, an *epos*; and then return again to a world not quite like the original one, but on another level."[13] Upon completion of their quests Thomas' heroes always seem about to set out again to repeat the action in a world only slightly altered, where the eternal progression of birth out of death, creation out of destruction, is more absolute than any final stasis.

In the more sombre early tales Thomas, like Blake,

brings Satan into the light of day to preside over the renewal of a life-cycle. From his earliest teens he had associated witchcraft and satanic lore with his own dark moods, making them vehicles of a negation of vitality which one might define as a negative organicism. As early as 1931 he ranks himself with the damned:

Children of darkness got no wings,
This we know we got no wings,
Stay, in a circle chalked upon the floor
Waiting all vainly this we know . . .[14]

taking upon himself the burden of Faust in a bitter parody of the Negro Cockaigne song, "All God's Chillun Got Wings." When he darkens the world of the early prose, he calls upon the traditions of demonology and witchery to describe the practice of the black art of mastery over life and death. The purpose of this tradition, writes Charles Williams, "is to discover or create an organic relationship other than the organic relationship which exists in the divine principles of the universe. The Devil desires, against those principles, to be an utter organic source; the witch desires to relate herself to the Devil as father and source."[15] This is, then, primitivism fallen through pride, naturalism perverted in the service of *hubris*. "It was a beautiful day in the rivers of the sun," exults Thomas in "The Orchards": Amabel Owen[16] of the unfinished *A Doom on the Sun* and the doctor's daughter of "The School for Witches" pervert Marlais' quest for the Logos in their attempts at union with a demonic power.

The two surviving chapters of *A Doom on the*

Sun, "The Enemies" and "The Holy Six," seem to depend, nonetheless, upon both negative and positive organicism, upon both the sabbatic traditions and the delightful apocalypses of Blake. The countryside is once more the anatomical Jarvis Valley, feminine in its contour: the Reverend Mr. Davies is drawn over "the breasts of the Jarvis hills" towards Mrs. Owen at the center of the valley. Could this be a parody on Rev. Edward Davies (of *Mythology and Rites*), hoist on his own syncretism, pitched headlong into the bosom of the White Goddess? "Loving his parish, he had loved the surrounding lands, but the hills had given under his feet or plunged him into the air. And, loving his God, he had loved the darkness where men of old had worshipped the dark invisible" (*AST*, p. 69).[17] The wind roars and whirls around the sides of the bowl-shaped valley, but the farmhouse is its still center, dominated by "an uncanny woman" in tune with "the old powers" of the universe.

In league with this spiderlike female is Mr. Owen, an outdoor man at work on a Blakean garden. His animated world must submit to his tortures: the weeds scream and bleed while he pulls at their "flesh of green grass," and the worms are jerked out of the ground like weeds. In the proper demonic fashion, Mr. Owen has subjugated the "organic source" of life to his mastery. The "vegetable world" roars at his feet as he presides over reproduction and death: "Multiply, multiply, he had said to the worms disturbed in their channelling, and had cut the brown worms in half so that the halves might breed and spread their life over the garden and go out, contaminating, into the fields and the bellies of the cattle" (*AST*, p. 67). Owen's world is the same as Thel's grave-pit and Peter's Jarvis valley, a world so powerful that it sucks the tottering representative of Welsh piety into its processes. As Jacob Korg has pointed out, the conflict between the Owens and Mr. Davies is a pathetic warfare between sterile religious morality and fertility, repression and passion.[18]   This is the same murderous struggle of sick reason and repressed passion which underlies Blake's poetry.

The sequel to "The Enemies" deals with a "black coming" brought about by six clergymen, whose names are anagrams on lust, greed, envy, cruelty, spite, and fear.[19]   These are the "Holy Six of Wales," perverted clergymen who seem to be in parody of the holy threes (triads) and sixes of which the bardic aphorisms were composed.   The clergymen follow Davies into a country alive with sensuality, where their own constant preoccupation with sex ("the Holy life was a constant erection") is manifest in a landscape tense with copulation.   As in "The Orchards" and "The Visitor" the countryside also participates in a bardic vitality: "There were six vowels in the language of the branches.   Old Vole [Love, the cart driver] heard the leaves."   Mrs. Owen, who "like Peter the poet, wrote of the Jarvis valley," bears a foetus which is the "last man's-word" created by "the world of light, and the holy Jewish Word."

The structure of "The Holy Six" depends upon

the six movements of a weird ritual. Each of the clergy approaches Amabel and, while his feet are being washed by Davies, crosses over the witches' circle which is drawn around her. This action is at the same time sexual and sabbatic: Mr. Vyne, for example, "sighed behind Mary and caught his breath at the seedy rim of the circle, seeing how beautiful she was as she shifted about him in the mothering middle of the earth" (AST, p. 138). Davies, now "three parts ghost," is the medium through which each of the six achieves his obeisance: "Hand in hand with the grey ghost," Mr. Stul "kissed on divinity until the heavens melted."

In all of this the sensual imagery represents the results of repressive religion, a conflict, as Jacob Korg describes it, between sterile religious morality and fertility, repression and passion, which resolves into a marriage of Blakean contraries. It is Mr. Rafe, apparently representing Blake's Urizenic evil of faintheartedness, who finds himself battling a voice from the Prophetic Books: "Ah, ah, oh, ah, cried the voice of Jerusalem, and Mary, from the moon's arc over the hill, ran like a wolf at the wailing ministers" (AST, p. 139). Mrs. Owen represents a variation on Albion's fallen emanation: "wise to the impious systems, [she] saw through the inner eye that the round but unbounded earth rotted as she ripened; a circle, not of her witch's making, grew around her; the immaculate circle broadened, taking a generation's shape" (AST, p. 137). In "The Holy Six" Thomas is ironic and prophetic, using witch-craft both as a satiric comment upon religious moralism and as a dark mode of participating in the creative cycles of the universe. In Amabel Owen's powerful person, "dead Mary" (the mother of Christ?) can be mounted to set in motion a new supernatural "coming" like that of the sexual Shiloh and his Shekinah or of Christ with his church in the last days.

Like Thomas' other prose heroes, Davies seeks a consort through whom his desires are expanded into mythological acts. In both his poetry and his prose Thomas' struggle for personal integrity is similarly complicated by his need for and alienation from his feminine counterpart, whom he cannot live without but who can be the most uncomfortable of bedfellows. We have seen how, in "An Adventure from a Work in Progress" and "In the Direction of the Beginning," a heroine is sought by a hero in an ark or cockle boat. The breeding island of "The Map of Love" and "My world is pyramid" is her appropriate abode: she stands on its erotic peak in the midst of a cleaving landscape. The hero conquers his opponent and takes her vital substance as his reward— we have seen how she degenerates into a "white pool" as her island crumbles into a new cycle of division and generation. In a number of poems, some begun in 1933 and 1934 and all finished between 1935 and 1941—"Where once the waters of your face," "Grief thief of time," "I make this in a warring absence," "Into her Lying Down Head," "Not from this anger," and "Unluckily for a Death" —the narrator is seeking relationship with a similar consort.

"Altarwise by owl-light," which Thomas worked on between December 1935 and July 1936, should be associated with such tales as "The Lemon" (1936), "The Orchards" (1934, 1936), "The Horse's Ha" (1935–1936), "The School for Witches" (1934?), and particularly the two fragments (published 1938, 1939). The narrative line seems to depend in part upon a quest for androgynous union: Christ ("the long world's gentleman," "the gentleman of wounds") has intercourse with "The long wound's woman," who is both Medusa and "God's Mary." Thus in the next to last sonnet Thomas

Weds my long gentleman to dusts and furies;
With priest and pharoah bed my gentle wound,
World in the sand, on the triangle landscape.
(CP, p. 85)[20]

This androgynous version of the trinity, which is very similar to the sexual consummations of "In the Direction of the Beginning" and "An Adventure from a Work in Progress," leads as in "The Map of Love" and "A Prospect of the Sea" to a new life-cycle. In the last sonnet the prophetic "bible fish" reports a new "flying garden" sown "round that sea-ghost," "Green as beginning." The hero of the sonnet sequence follows the same quest as Marlais, the hero of "The Mouse and the Woman," the Noah of the fragments, and the fisher of the "Ballad of the Long-legged Bait" toward the same paradoxical goal.

In his study of witchcraft Charles Williams describes "a tradition of great and awful blasphemy—the sexual union of alien and opposed natures."[21]

In "The Holy Six," Davies, who is a "ghost," mounts Amabel, who is very much alive. In some of the poems written during the same period as the *Doom on the Sun* stories, Thomas deals with a modern version of this diabolical union—a wedding of the world of dead objects to the world of living subjects. In the second section of "All all and all the dry worlds lever" the flesh becomes wed to machines, the blood "synthetic," and the heart incarnate in "ribbing metal." Like Peter who in "The Visitor" struggles against the clockwork objectification of his personality, the poet battles machines only, at the end, to affirm their role as one of the contraries of existence:

All all and all the dry worlds couple

. . . .

Stroke of mechanical flesh on mine
Square in these worlds the mortal circle.

(CP, p. 39)

The imagery of the first section of "I, in my intricate image" establishes the paradox of metal object and organic subject which again is the central concern. Thomas poses a riddle which asks what could be both "mortal, unmortal," wood and metal, a "fusion of rose and male motion." The answer, supported by the suggestion of voyage and return reminiscent of Donne's "A Valediction: forbidding mourning," is probably "a compass." This instrument is made of pencil and steel, wood and metal, combining erection with a circling motion which indeed produces roselike patterns. As a sexual symbol, it is analogous to the "steeplejack tower, bone-railed and masterless" of the male phallus. An instrument of both life and death, the "sea-spindle lateral" is a "stylus of lightning" held by the creator and, in the parenthetical verses of the second section, an instrument of death or at least of radical surgery.

All of this paradoxical imagery coalesces when Thomas-the-narrator-hero confronts the crocodile, a hideous embodiment of armor and flesh, associated in Egyptian religion with absolute dismemberment and death.[22] As the world looks on at the modern Galahad, he not only destroys the dragon but absorbs its nature:

And, as for oils and ointments on the flying grail,
All-hollowed man wept for his white apparel.

Man was Cadaver's masker, the harnessing mantle,
Windily master of man was the rotten fathom,
My ghost in his metal neptune
Forged in man's mineral.

(*CP*, p. 44)

Thomas is once more describing a wedding of opposite natures such as occurs at the end of "The Holy Six," "The Lemon," and "The Visitor," which, along with "The School for Witches," contain the most thorough working out of this antithesis. In both his poetry and his prose he frequently uses images of metal to represent death or objectivity in conflict with the softer and more subjective images of flesh and plant life. This marriage of metal and wood or metal and flesh seems to be a Blakean confrontation between the "Satanic Mills" and the "human form divine" brought into the contemporary setting of conflict between man and machine. As in Blake's progression of contraries, the battle leads from division and clash to a new synthesis.

Where in "The Lemon" surgery is set against natural growth and science is set against dream—in a battle which culminates when Nant cuts the lemon in half with the goddess' scissors—in "The School for Witches" it is three tinkers, or workers-in-metal, who culminate a sexual rite of the new year. The witch, who is a sister to Amabel Owen and the heroines of "In the Direction of the Beginning" and "An Adventure from a Work in Progress," is also in league with the powers "swarming under the west roots." Her desire for the devil and the rites with which she summons him are appropriate to orthodox witchcraft as expounded by Miss Murray. "Still untaken," Thomas' witch instructs "seven country girls" in the methods of raising the devil, to which end the medium of actual human males is essential. In the eyes of her familiar[23] she reads the news "of a great and unholy coming" of "a beast in stag's skin." This antlered animal resembles the figure whom Miss Murray hails as the horned divinity of the "old religion" of Britain. Thomas' seven girls could represent the seven maidens involved in the rite of the new year;[24] the action, which takes place on "the first evening of the new year," is completed by the arrival of a black baby who hails a new infernal cycle.

The child is born to a mad Negress attended by the doctor and a midwife near a country asylum.

They journey to the birth in a "solid darkness" to assist at a "black birth" in a Jarvis valley where death and reproduction carry on their contrary dance. At the same instant that the child is born, three tinkers, their paths crossed by a black cat, are drawn to the witch's tower. "Tom the scissorman" takes on the persona of the horned demon lover while "John Bucket" and the "panman" are drawn into a dance around his mating with the doctor's daughter. As the doctor and midwife carry the child in, the black epiphany is completed while the dancers, having achieved the proper quorum of thirteen, cry "a coven, a coven."

The going-out of doctor and midwife, the gathering in of the Satan-man and his fellow tinkers, and the achievement of the coven circle constitute three movements in a sabbatic rite of the new year. Like the Holy Six and Gaspar, Melchior, and Balthasar, the three tinkers are ironic prototypes—here of the wise men who sought the newborn Christ. The blackness of the tale is bright with a dark gaiety as if Thomas were parodying the deadpan horrors of Machen and Huysmans, a whimsical mood which evaporates in his grimmest tales.

IV

In the first poem of the February 1933 Notebook Thomas declares that he has become "the night's friend, / Friend of the grave, grave friend," familiar with the decay of the flesh to the extent that "companionship with the night has turned / Each ugly corpse into a friend."[25] He never reworked such maudlin and repetitive verses for publication, but something of their mood sustains two of his harshest tales, "The Horse's Ha" and "The Burning Baby." Evil, which is colored "green as the woman's eyes and blacker than the shadows pouched under the lower lids" in the *Doom on the Sun* stories and bright black in "The School for Witches," is colored white in "The Horse's Ha." The white horse brings the dead-white apocalypse of cancer to a tale filled with images of sallow flesh swollen with living death.

The "ha" is the horselaugh of death, although Thomas could have had in mind the cry of "hou, haru, har" with which Cornish witches summon the devil.[26] The horse could be the white horse revered in certain parts of pagan Britain (or the one on the whiskey bottle?).[27] Keeping a dead body alive, one mode of creating an organic relationship hateful to God, was an end in itself to the demonic practitioner. The nightmare of the white plague in "The Horse's Ha" is worse than death, since the entire population of "Cathmarw" (Welsh for "death") wanders around in a living death, awaiting measurement and burial.

The undertaker keeps himself alive by brewing a "resurrection cup" from the recipe of his mother Bronwen, whose name Thomas seems to have taken from Branwen, heroine of the *Mabinogion* tale of "Branwen, Daughter of Llyr." By drinking his brew of parson's semen and other appropriate ingredients, Montgomery the undertaker leads the unhappy dead, caught in the postures of their love-making and daily occupations, to the edge of the grave. Each victim of the plague, brooding about his experience, asks a riddle of death appropriate to his calling. ApLlewelyn the organist wants to know, "What is death's music, one note or many?" His pet starlings had been killed by Montgomery but, like Hardy, he blames the indifference of God: "He who marks the sparrow's fall has no time for my birds." The parson asks "What is God's death?" but his only answer is that God "took my promise" of semen. Thomas' deity, like Hardy's, exists only to be disinterested; his deism, like his father's, "had nothing to do with whether there was a God or not."[28]

The coming of the white horse, the spread of the plague, and the burial of the villagers are three movements in a litany of total despair. Because of the structure and craft with which Thomas develops his ritual there is nothing tawdry in his expression. Where "The Holy Six" ends with Davies' question whether "the faces of the West stars are the backs of the East," in "The Horse's Ha" Thomas concludes that "One by one the stars went out, leaving a hole in heaven."

Because of its dependence upon human action rather than upon the inhuman force of plague, "The Burning Baby" is even more terrifying than "The Horse's Ha." Evil in this tale is painted a fiery red: the parson Rhys Rhys falls in love with his daughter as the midsummer gorse catches fire (at the August Albans); her flesh is "red with the smoothing of his hand"; she dies "in a gown of blood" after bearing a dead son; her changeling brother wears a red coat and fondles a bloody rabbit. According to Glyn Jones, Thomas got the idea for this story from an event of January 13, 1884, when the Reverend Dr. Price of Llantrisant burned an infant son whom he had named "Jesus Christ."[29] Rhys Rhys' love for his daughter is an even more bitter parody of the Christian incarnation.

The burning of victims was the druid mode of capital punishment: by submitting themselves to the fire even murderers could be purged by divine light and spared utter death. Rhys Rhys gathers heather faggots in "a circle" (which in an earlier draft was "a druid circle")[30] and as the immolation takes place he throws up his hands to pray "before the red eye of the creeping fire." The rite of Rhys Rhys and his dead child is a brutal reinterpretation of Abraham's attempted sacrifice of Isaac and of God's successful sacrifice of Christ.

The union of "ghost" Davies with Amabel Owen, the intercourse of the doctor's daughter with the scissorman-devil, the burial of the plague dead of Cathmarw, and the burning of Rhys Rhys' baby are as much climaxes of inward psychological pilgrimages as are the ritual denouements of "The Map of Love," "A Prospect of the Sea," and "The Orchards." In the brighter tales, love and vision come to the heroes through an unconscious providence, while in the darker ones the heroes more consciously manipulate the powers of birth, life, and death. Both are ritual dramatizations of the poet's quest for creative power and of man's perennial attempt to make a living reality out of abstract doctrine.

V

The fundamental difference between Christianity and the "old religion," writes Miss Murray, is "that the Christian believes that God died once for all, whereas the more primitive belief is that the god is perpetually incarnate on earth and may therefore be put to death over and over again."[31] We have seen in Chapter 3 that Thomas' Christ, like the Christ of Welsh theology, remains in Abred, and that Thomas himself belongs to the more primitive of the two traditions. In a January 1934 note to Trevor Hughes accompanying "Before I knocked," "My hero bares his nerves," "Light breaks where no sun shines," and "I fellowed sleep," Thomas defends "the diction, the perhaps wearisome succession of blood and bones, the never ending similes of the streams of the veins and the lights in the eyes, by saying that, for the time at least, I realise that it is impossible for me to raise myself to the altitude of the stars, and that I am forced, therefore, to bring down the stars to my own level and to incorporate them in my own physical universe."[32] "No man can live," he proclaims in a 1933 Notebook poem,

Who does not bury god in a deep grave
And then raise up the skeleton again,
No man who does not break and make,
Who in the bones finds not new faith,
Lends not flesh to ribs and neck,
Who does not break and make his final faith.[33]

Thomas is constantly killing god and then raising him up again in both his prose and poetry, breaking down old abstractions of doctrine and reconstructing something fresh and no less divine. "I must create a System or be enslaved by another Man's," declares Blake's Los, "I will not Reason & Compare: my business is to Create."[34]

In the title poem to *The World I Breathe* ("Today, this insect," originally in the 1930–1932 Notebook), Thomas explains why he chose sometimes to portray the process of creation in a dark and sometimes in a bright mood. "The insect certain is the plague of fables," he announces: any well-constructed personal myth must be paradoxical since to Thomas as to Blake contraries are essential to human existence. The insect might be the Egyptian scarab, which lays its egg on a pile of dung, but from the text it seems more like Owen's worm, a creature which "measures his own length on the garden wall / And breaks his shell in the last shocked beginning."[35] In an engraving entitled "Glad Day" Blake draws Albion naked in a blaze of sunlight, with a caterpillar or chrysalis beneath his left foot and a mothlike creature flying up from the earth between his legs.[36] The inauguration of the new cycle is a "shocked beginning" because of the dark division which precedes it:

In trust and tale have I divided sense,
Slapped down the guillotine, the blood-red double
Of head and tail made witnesses to this
Murder of Eden and green genesis.

(CP, p. 47)

"Division of the senses" is part of Blake's fortunate fall: Thomas, like Owen, cuts the worm in two so that both contamination and reproduction may go on. In some of the tales he attacks the universe until the sun is doomed and the stars go out so that only through the "hole in heaven" can divinity be resurrected.

During the visit to Llangain in Carmarthenshire during September 1933, Thomas wrote down two poems which are distinctly Blakean. The first, an entry of September 12, 1933 in the August 1933 Notebook, is modeled upon Blake's "Mental Traveller" in both style and conception. In the second Thomas defined the place of such tales as "The Horse's Ha" in his universe:

A hole in space shall keep the shape of thought,
The lines of earth, the curving of the heart,
And from this darkness spin the golden soul.
Intangible, my world shall come to nought.
The solid world shall wither in the heat.
How soon, how soon, o Lord of the red hail![37]

As in the *Doom on the Sun* stories, "The Horse's Ha," "The Burning Baby," and "The School for Witches," darkness, "nought," and the arrival of an Antichrist precede the inauguration of a new world cycle. Built upon what Northrop Frye describes as the cyclical rhythms of "light and darkness," "waking and dreaming life," "innocence and experience," Thomas' darker tales are apocalytic in conception. As always in his work, their images depend upon a "sequence of creations, recreations, destructions, contradictions" which derive from an internal personal battle of "a beast, an angel, and a madman."[38]

His demonic tales are built upon such unresolved Blakean "contraries" as energy and repression, vitality and decay. The birth impending at each denouement implies the renewal of a cycle not bounded by witchcraft, since it is the "immaculate circle" of apocalyptic destruction and regeneration. The resolution of the conflicts of one cycle and the inauguration of new antitheses is implicit at each denouement, where the cut worm gets his tail in his mouth so that "blind in the coil scrams round the blazing outline" (*CP*, p. 47).

CHAPTER V

Surrealism as a Literary Method

*"But now we turn to the dream with the same confidence that for-
merly men placed in the objective world of sensation, and we weave
its reality into the synthesis of our art. It is possible that in the
integral dream—the dream as entire myth rather than as a series of
fragmentary symbols—the work of synthesis is already done."*

Herbert Read, Surrealism

From 1932, when an exhibition of Ernst and Miro
opened at the Mayer Gallery, until 1939 and the
outbreak of the Second World War, London found
itself in the unusual position of outpost of an international movement in iconoclastic art and poetry.
Surrealism, which had been born officially in France
with Breton's *Manifestos* of 1924 and 1930, moved
to England as conditions on the continent worsened.
The British, who had quite naturally remained un-
moved by the dadaists and whose reaction to the
shock of the First World War had taken the more
systematized forms of Wyndham Lewis' vorticism
and of W. H. R. Rivers' depth psychology, were
quick to respond to the carefully worked out doctrines of the surrealists. The philosophy and aesthetics of Breton and his followers were interpreted for
the British by the critic-poets David Gascoyne and

Herbert Read, whose works *A Short Survey of Surrealism* and *Surrealism* appeared in 1935 and 1936. The London Surrealist Exhibition opened at the New Burlington Galleries in June of 1936.

The most striking trait of surrealist art was a weird mingling of object and subject, of machine and flesh in an expression of both acceptance and distaste for the modern age. As John Bayley points out, the romantic theorists had made a similar attempt to bridge the objective and subjective poles of their world, an attempt which carried over into "the modern conception of art which is to create a suggestive magic including at the same time object and subject, the world outside the artist and the artist himself."[1] The surrealists shared with the romantics and the late nineteenth-century occultists a desire to bring together disparate forms of life, to find a "supreme point where all contradictions are reconciled," a place of quasi-demonic marriage which for the modern artist is to be found in the "untrammelled unconscious."[2]

Thomas' *18 Poems* manifests a predilection for verbal play, for erotic imagery, and Freudian motifs that is analogous to surrealist techniques. His *Twenty-Five Poems* includes poems-about-writing-poetry highly suggestive of the literary method expounded by Read and Gascoyne. As I noted in a previous chapter, Thomas struggled throughout his early and middle years with the relationship between metal and flesh, the modern age and poetic lyricism.

Thomas' affinity to the surrealist movement is

more than coincidental: that he was thoroughly acquainted with the surrealist literary theory is clear from his lucid critique of it in "Notes on the Art of Poetry."[3] It was into a literary London temporarily steeped in the surrealist mélange of erotic joke and metaphysical insanity that he plunged during his earliest London visits. As I noted in the Introduction, he attended the 1936 exhibit and was invited to give a reading with Eluard and others at a surrealist poetry gathering in July of the same year.[4] As we shall see in this chapter, a study of the first and last drafts of "The Orchards" reveals that between 1934 and 1936 he not only became aware of surrealist definitions of word, image, and dream but incorporated them into the text of his most complex early tales.

I

In his outline of the surrealist literary method Sir Herbert Read quotes Vico's *De Consonantia Philologiae* as a source for the surrealist linguistic theory. The poet, Vico had written, "must unlearn all his native language and return to the pristine beggary of words," a statement which Read compares to Freud's definition of a "primitive grammarless speech" in which "the abstract is merged again into the concrete from which it sprang."[5] The marriage of word and object occurs repeatedly in Thomas' early prose, as in "An Adventure from a Work in Progress" where "the history of the boat was spelt in knocking water" and "each syllable of the adventure struck on grass and stone" (*AST*, p. 154).[6] In several of the tales, as we have seen, the hero abandons verbal princesses and abstract fantasy for a more concrete embodiment of his desire. In his quest the "word" is a lively and autonomous entity which both accompanies and combats him. "He struggled with his words like a man with the sun," writes Thomas of Marlais in "The Orchards," and Peter, in "The Visitor," is involved in a battle of words: "He heard in his brain the voices of Callaghan and Rhianon battle until he slept, and tasted the blood of words" (*AST*, p. 78).

The search of Thomas' heroes for a primitive, living word occurs in conjunction with a quest for a pattern of words or a manner in which words can be knit together as images to form a visual structure. The surrealists turned to the dream as a model of literary technique, even coming to rely upon wholly "automatic" writing-out of the dreams. Although the result of this complete abrogation of conscious control was often ludicrous, their main point—that the world of the unconscious was a vital source of poetic imagery—could not have been more strongly made. The same Eden-morning enthusiasm about the unconscious as a source for literary inspiration was characteristic of Eugene Jolas' *transition*, which had its genesis in the French surrealist movement (see Appendix C). Whether Thomas' desire to describe and explore the world of dreams derived from the surrealists or from some other source, such as Walter de la Mare's *Behold This Dreamer*, in "The Orchards," "The Mouse and the Woman," and "The Lemon" he makes explicit use of dream as a pattern of images and symbols knit into a structure.

"The Lemon" is a complex rendering of the d_____ ing mind. The bulk of the tale takes place with_ Nant, a boy who is trying to wrest the power of life and death from the hands of his scientist-father, Dr. Manza. Manza, like Wells' Dr. Moreau, is engaged in artificial recreation of life by grafting one species upon another.[7] The atmosphere of scientific horror is the sterile hell of rationalism which was both feared and parodied by the surrealists, as by Blake. The tower-laboratory, full of inmates waiting to be "new born," sits on top of what seem to be the Jarvis hills. To Nant the entire place is the potent and enclosing symbol of his father, and although he knows its "name" he is at the outset uninitiated into its "one mystery." An analogous tower plays an important part in "The Tree," and in poems like "Ears in the turrets hear" and "Do you not father me."

In "The Lemon" the obviously Freudian plot is complicated by the splitting up of the point of view. At first Thomas describes the action from a removed vantage point but after establishing the setting he announces that "I was that boy in a dream." The boy in turn is split, accompanied by a "ghostly other" like the second voice of "I fellowed sleep." Nant is aware, in addition, of moving on several levels of the dream: "I knew that I was dreaming," he says, "but suddenly I awoke to the real, hard lack of light in the corridors of the house." From a mythological dream of burrowing under Wales he seems to waken to the Freudian struggle with the father.

Thomas is thus taking the point of view of himself-as-dreamer, himself-as-Nant, and himself-as-Nant's-double. The sensation of sitting "above" a dream as an onlooker while one's personality is split was described by Robert Graves in *The Meaning of Dreams*. Graves had learned from W. H. R. Rivers the classical Freudian manner in which the dreamer divides himself into distinct actors in order to express a conflict in the personality. Thomas divides himself into two motivational figures: one expressing desire for the father's power and the other desire to remain the obedient son. When Nant climbs the tower, kisses the woman in it, and eats the lemon Thomas stands aside from the consummation, determined to make his "own way, the way of light breaking over Cathmarw hill and the black valley." His implication is that, although he has burrowed into the collective unconscious and witnessed the rites of the Freudian unconscious, he is not bound by either but prefers to return to light and reason. "My poetry," he wrote in October 1934, "is useful to me for one reason: it is the record of my individual struggle from darkness towards some measure of light."[8] We saw in Chapter 2 how a similar journey through the waters of the unconscious and a quest for light provide the narrative structure of several early poems.

In "The Lemon," for all its complexity, Thomas is making his position on the literary use of the dream extremely clear. Later, when he came to evaluate the surrealist movement, he explained that "the Surrealists wanted to dive into the subconscious mind . . . and dig up images from there without the aid of logic or reason." "I do not mind," he concludes, "from where the images of a poem are dragged up; drag them up, if you like, from the nethermost sea of the hidden self; but, before they reach paper, they must go through all the rational processes of the intellect."[9] Even in his early tales Thomas sifts and arranges a chaotic wealth of unconscious material according to the rules of narrative coherence.

In defining surrealism as "the most important literary influence which the stories [in *The World I Breathe*] manifest," Jacob Korg notes that Thomas' "central device [is] that of interpreting the physical world according to the standards of irrational mental states identical with the 'paranoical activity' offered as an artistic method by Salvador Dali."[10] In one of his manifestos Breton provides a "recipe" for such writing: "The cave-bear and the lout his companion, the vol-au-vent and the wind his valet, the Lord High Chancellor and his wife, the sparrow-scarer and the old fellow his compeers, the test-tube and her daughter the needle, the cannibal and his brother the carnival . . . have nothing to do than to disappear from the surface of the sea."[11] The passage depends upon the arbitrary verbal associations cast forth by the dreaming mind—Freud's "primitive grammarless speech." In describing the storm that goes on in the "exterior" world all through "The Lemon" Thomas makes similar use of catalogues and verbal play: "The storm, the black man, the whistler from the sea bottom . . . , the thunder, the lightning, the mighty pebbles, these came up; as a sickness, an afterbirth, coming up from the belly of weathers . . . a sea of flame or a steam crucifix, . . . the whole, the unholy, rock handed, came up coming up" (*AST*, p. 87–88). The images are drawn together not by their philological similarity but by their participation in a storm of birth out of childhood which underlines the central theme of the tale. In both its imagery and its action the passage forms an integral part of the plot.

"The Orchards," like Thomas' later "Notes on the Art of Poetry," is a critique of surrealism and an analysis of the proper use of its materials. It is carefully constructed upon a pattern of dreaming, writing-out of the dream, dreaming again, and a final quest for the source of the dream. The dream at the core of the story consists of two scenes made up of related images: first the orchard on fire, with flames shooting up through the blossoms in a manner reminiscent of Blake's drawings; then a vision of the young and beautiful maiden pointing to the charred trees and to her "scarecrow sister," whom Marlais must kiss as the fires die. The second scene describes the role which the dreamer must play within the context of the first: it suggests thus the latent realization of the manifest dream-content.[12] With the hero of "The Lemon" he moves out of the unconscious into a "real" light which, like Peter's valley, devours as it regenerates. By taking the dream-symbols to himself in his "folkwalk" Marlais will renew the numinous flames of death and rebirth within his own personality.

Marlais' reaction upon awaking is one of recognition of his latent involvement in the dream scene:

the women, he realizes, "were his scarecrow lovers
forever and ever." Looking out from his city window he is conscious of the existence of actual orchards "a dozen valleys away." He nonetheless lingers
in an attempt to verbalize the dream, and the result
is an example of automatic writing: "Put a two-
coloured ring of two women's hair round the blue
world, white and coal-black against the summer-
coloured boundaries of sky and grass, four-breasted
stems at the poles of the summer sea-ends, eyes in
the sea-shells, two fruit trees out of a coal-hill; poor
Marlais' morning . . . spins before you" (*AST*, p. 98).
This passage (which represents what Kenneth Burke
calls the "gargoyle thinking" of surrealism) was
pounced upon by one critic who considered its
"vague Picassoan outré-ness" and "vague Daliesque
thrill" typical of the negative effect that surrealism
was having upon Thomas.[13]

What the critic missed by not reading "The Orchards" more carefully was the fact that in this particular passage Thomas was *parodying* the surrealist
method as a style which drives the hero to despair
that "the word is too much with us." The echo of
Wordsworth's sonnet "The World is too Much With
Us" is not accidental: Marlais is moved by a romantic desire to find renewal in "Nature" and to "have
sight of Proteus rising from the sea." Thomas copied
out in the Red Notebook in 1934 the first and much
briefer version of the story, entitled first "Mr. Tritas
on the Roofs" and later "Anagram." The early tale
describes the walk of a frustrated writer upon the
London roofs (in "The Orchards" the setting is prob-

ably Swansea) where, like Marlais, he seeks the source of all images. He does not dream, but gazes at the moon and broods about lunar women.

"The End of the River," like "Anagram" seems to have been written in 1934—it was listed, although not copied, in the Red Notebook and appeared on November 22, 1934, in the *New English Weekly*. Here again we see the outline of "The Orchards" in skeleton: Sir Peregrine, the twelfth baron of Quincey, decides to end his wasted line by walking to the end of the river which winds through his property ("The end of the world," he realizes, "was the end of the river"). As in "The Tree," there is an omniscient gardener, Chubb, who in his mysterious control over events resembles Sam Rib of "The Map of Love," Manza of "The Lemon," and Owen of "The Enemies" and "The Holy Six." Sir Peregrine, having made his decision, runs through field after field along the river, passing "A crow, perched on a scarecrow's shoulder" and coming at last to a "girl-child" washing clothes who "with a frightened cry . . . thrust an unwashed napkin [British for diaper] into his hand."[14]

The basic difference between "Anagram," "The End of the River," and "The Orchards" is that in the first two we have the bare outlines of the more richly developed structure of the final piece. By 1936, when Thomas revised "Anagram" for publication, he was sufficiently aware of surrealism not only to parody it but to improve upon its methods. This was the same year that "The Mouse and the Woman" was finished for *transition*, which several years before had included among its contributions notes on dreams ("I am a dream-man in a chaos," declared Eugene Jolas[15]); reworkings of primitive fables ("Day and Night, a Yoruba Folktale," "Two Cuban Negro Prayers,"[16] "The Forsaken Merman"[17]); and accounts of the progression of insanity ("Illustrations of madness,"[18] "The Death of 21 Years"[19]). I would conclude that between 1934 and 1936, the period when most of the early prose was completed for publication, Thomas became interested in the use of dream as a source of imagery and sought to redefine his art as an improvement upon the literary methods of the surrealist movement in England.

II

With their emphasis on Freud and the dream it was inevitable that the surrealists should also be fascinated by insanity. Under the influence of Salvador Dali's "simulations of various types of mental disease" the distortion of the objective world by the pressure of the mad mind became a model of artistic structure. "Within his head revolved a little world," wrote Thomas of the madman-hero of a long ballad written in April 1933. In their ability to construct new worlds out of their heads Thomas' madmen become "worldmen," suffering and triumphing with the archetypal hero:

So crying, he was pushed into the Jordan,
He, too, has known the agony in the garden
And felt a skewer enter in his side.[20]

"Hallucination," writes Paul Ray, "is the key word for those of Thomas' stories that bear the surrealist

stamp."[21]   Drawing upon several seminal poems
from the 1933 Notebook, Thomas used hallucination
as a literary technique in a number of his early tales.

"The Dress," "The Vest," and "The True Story"
(the first two entered in the Red Notebook in 1934,
the third published in 1939) are straightforward
tales in the manner of "thrillers," written from the
point of view of one intimate with the world of the
protagonists but not caught up in it.   In "The Dress"
a madman is searching for a woman whom he has
mutilated.   As he is fleeing from his wardens another young woman is trying on a new dress.   The
madman wanders through the woods, hugging nature to himself in the same way that the idiot of
"The Tree" "brothered" the wind and the rain.
Mental debility, in Thomas' world, makes the natural
landscape not only a metaphor but an actual extension of the human body.   This landscape is probably
the Jarvis countryside: the madman shakes off his
pursuers at the foot of what seem to be the Jarvis
hills and makes his way to the garden and cottage
where a pregnant young woman awaits her husband.

The landscape is distorted according to his mental
turmoil: exactly as it rocked beneath Davies in "The
Enemies" the Jarvis valley streams and billows
around the madman until it shrinks into a ball beneath his feet.   Calling himself a "son of woman,"
the madman is not unlike Marlais, the folkman walking, with the world rolling beneath his feet.   Because
of the sadism of the madman's original crime—the
cutting off of his wife's lips for infidelity—the reader
expects a sensational denouement.   Thomas con-

cludes, however, with a lyrically simple act in the manner of "The Orchards" and "The Map of Love": "She sat before him, covered in flowers. Sleep, said the madman. And, kneeling down, he put his bewildered head upon her lap" (*AST*, p. 168).

On the Freudian level, the madman is fleeing the world to the lap of his mother-lover. He joins Nant, Davies, Marlais, and the heroes of the two fragmentary tales in his quest for the woman who bestows life and death simultaneously upon the adventurer. Where in "The Orchards" and "The Lemon" the feminine symbol arises out of the world of dream, she is brought into being in "The Dress" by a conjunction of hallucination and reality.

"The Vest" and "The True Story," although finished, craftsmanlike pieces, may be taken as horror stories on a more straightforward level. The first deals with a man driven mad by the thought of death. His fear is brought to a violent head by the sight of a dead dog, and his defensive reaction to his fear is to mutilate his wife. In an earlier version of the tale Thomas described the hero as a killer walking the streets after the murder, trying to enter a number of bars and night spots. "What would the Swansea streets look like," Thomas seems to be asking, "to a man who had just slaughtered his wife?" In the final version the hero enters only one bar, where he exhibits the bloody vest of his wife.

In "The True Story" Thomas describes the state of mind of a young girl who has killed an old woman in her charge. Having failed to persuade the boy-servant to help bury the body even by offering him her own, she commits suicide by "flying" out of the window. The narrative is clearly Freudian, the girl's desire for sexual freedom being expressed in the murder of the miserly old woman and seduction of the boy. The girl, who had never left the house save to pick berries and to slaughter chickens, seems to be another prototype of Thomas' woman of fruition and death. He remains wholly the omniscient narrator, concluding smugly with the statement "But Martha was not flying." "After the Fair," entered in the Red Notebook in 1933, is a similarly straightforward story of a young mother, who comes upon a fat man at a fair and takes her fatherless child for an endless ride on the merry-go-round ("roundabout"). Her name is Annie, and she is perhaps a more orthodox version of Amabel Owen, heroine of the *Doom on the Sun* stories which Thomas was composing at the same time.

In "The Mouse and the Woman,"[22] which was probably begun in 1932 and finished in 1936, Thomas' narrative no longer deals with madness from one removed. It embodies the whirl of dream, hallucination, and reality in the mind of a poet who must confront his own unconscious. The tale is arranged in numbered sections, the first, twelfth, and last representing the present and those in between representing events leading up to the hero's insanity. In several of the later sections, where he assumes the point of view of his hero, Thomas writes in the language and symbolism of insanity.

The cause of the poet-hero's madness is the kind of prudery that Blake condemned in his *Prophetic*

Books. Going against Blake's aphorism that "the nakedness of woman is the work of god," he loses touch with a part of his own personality. Above all things, Blake had feared and despised what Freud was to define as "repression": "He who desires but acts not," he asserted, "breeds pestilence." When Tharmas, the hero of the "Four Zoäs," rejects his "emanation" or female consort, eternity is shattered into the cycle of the temporal seasons. The androgynous union of man and woman in the garden of Eden is replaced by the alternation of innocence and experience, spring and fall, birth and death. Until Tharmas can accept these "contraries" as ultimately redemptive he is condemned to a conflict between his faculties of imagination (Los), desire (Luvah) and reason (Urizen). In "The Mouse and the Woman" the hero rejects a consort who "had been with him from the beginning," casting out with her "the rhythm of the old figures' moving, the spring trot, summer canter, sad stride of autumn, and winter shuffle" (*AST*, p. 116–117). In trying to make a cripple of the god of the seasons he cripples his own personality.

The events of the tale spring from a dream which the hero brings into actual life. It falls into two distinct parts, the first dominated by "seven women, in a mad play by a Greek"—probably referring to *Elektra*, which Thomas saw performed in 1933—and the second by "an avenue of trees" which "leant forward and interlaced their hands, turning into a black forest." The seven women are all aspects of one unborn woman, crying from within the poet to be brought to life. In the dream the women are transformed into a forest which, in reverse of Marlais' redemptive orchard, is a place where the hero feels "absurd in his nakedness." He tries to forget the woman who had "risen out of the depths of darkness" but is unable to divorce himself from her: "She had moved in his belly when he was a boy, and stirred in his boy's loins." Compelled to acknowledge this sister or double he takes a surrealist plunge into the unconscious world: "He could no longer listen to the speaking of reason. The pulse of a new heart beat at his side. Contentedly he let the dream dictate its rhythm" (*AST*, p. 106).

As the woman comes alive to live with the poet, the dream world is wed to reality. He is still unable to accept her, however, for in the night after her birth he dreams a dream full of snakes and the wrath of a father-god with phallic mice in his beard. He sees himself as an airman (apparently crashed), "a foetus in a bottle," and a mousetrap—all stock symbols of castration. The dream finally dissolves into a dislocated jargon similar to Freud's "primitive, grammarless speech": "He could remember little else except the odds and ends of sentences, the movement of a turning shoulder, the sudden flight or drop of syllables" (*AST*, p. 110–111). Here, as in "The Orchards," the incursion of surrealistic passages represents abandonment of rational control and a lapse into artistic sterility.

The events succeeding the dream fulfill its portent. The following night, as the hero and his consort achieve a sexual consummation, a mouse comes out of its hole. On the Freudian level this creature suggests detumescence, although in *The Golden Bough* Frazer describes it as a symbol of the soul escaping from the mouth in sleep.[23] Thomas uses it in both senses in "Lament," a later poem where "At last the soul from its foul mouse hole / Slunk pouting out when the limp time came." For Thomas, who loathed mice and moralism, the mouse in "The Mouse and the Woman" represents a negative attitude towards the innocent sensualism of the heroine. In rejecting the woman because her nakedness "is not good to look upon" the poet makes her fade back into unreality, falling himself into a state of grief where he has a second dream of impotency. In section eighteen, Thomas takes over his point of view, plunging into a mad argument with the sun deity and god of the seasons. As we have seen, in his madness the hero contends with the Egyptian dog star and a Mosaic Jehovah. Unable to stand against the laws governing both the universe and the human personality he crumbles into total insanity, oblivious even to the arrival of spring.

The plot of "The Mouse and the Woman" may have originated in poems 3, 17, and 24 in the February 1933 Notebook—poems written during one of Thomas' early periods of gloom. These poems describe madness as a state of adolescent guilt in which the beauty of sexual love has been tarnished by shame. The first entry describes a woman who has loved the poet "from the beginning." Had she not loved him, muses Thomas, "my hand would not have changed to snakes." The ballad is a fairly complex account of madness. For the poet-hero

All reason broke, and horror walked the roads
A smile let loose a devil, a bell struck.
He could hear women breathing in the dark,
See women's faces under living snoods,
With serpents' mouths and scalecaphidian voids
Where eyes should be, and nostrils full of toads.[24]

III

By 1936 Thomas had brought to this raw material a more sophisticated literary method. The surrealist image, writes Paul Ray, was "a verbal transcription of an interior landscape, as opposed to the traditional image which transcribes an exterior landscape."[25] Fascinated by the film medium, the surrealists took advantage of its abolition of usual transitions to create unusual connections between disparate groups of images. Film techniques were carried over into surrealist fiction where, as in the case of Georges Ribemont-Dessaignes' "The Eighth Day of the Week," the author speaks with the abbreviated precision of the film director rather than with the more conventional narrative voice.[26] As we saw in Chapter 1, Thomas' prose was characterized from the earliest entry in the Red Notebook by a conflict and synthesis of thematic imagery accompanying the narrative line. In "The Lemon" and "The Mouse and the Woman," however, his usual adherence to an explicit narrative pattern gives way to a shifting of scenes from one aspect of the protagonist's mental state to another. In a manner not dissimilar from that of a film scenario, in "The Lemon" he announces of one series of images that "This was the exterior world" and later of another that "This was the dance of celebration in the interior world." (He was later to write a number of film adaptations including *The Doctor and the Devils* and *The Beach of Falesá.*[27]) In "The Mouse and the Woman" the sections are numbered in a manner characteristic of several contributions to *transition* which deal with insanity.[28] The sections take us back and forth between images of past and present, dream, waking, and madness. As the hero's madness deepens the sections are characterized by more and more imagery with less and less narrative connection until his mind gives way to a massive confusion of mythological and Freudian symbols.

The continental surrealists were convinced that the artist should abandon rational control to plunge into the masterful world of the underground personality. The English surrealists were slightly more moderate, with Read emphasizing a Coleridgian balance between fancy and reason. Thomas "profoundly disagreed" with the ultimate aim of the continental movement, which was a psychological utopia attainable to anyone who could give his mind over to revery, hallucination, and dream.[29] He was concerned with exploring the unconscious mind, and he found there not a facile release but the challenge of two warring worlds. The heroes of "The Orchards," "The Dress," "The Vest," "The True Story," "The Mouse and the Woman," and "The Lemon"

all try to live with the dominant figures of their sub-
terranean or "surreal" personalities, but Marlais and
the hero of "The Lemon" are the only ones to confront the depths and remain sane. Thomas' relationship to the surrealist movement is clearly that
of a critic in the deepest sense: sympathetic to the
use of image, symbol, and plot derived from hallucination and the dream, he brought these elements
together in tales which embody man's search for a
relationship between the conscious and unconscious
worlds.

CHAPTER VI

The Later Prose
and Narrative Poetry

I have been, and I have returned.
I have mounted up on the wings of the morning,
    and I have dredged down to the zenith's reversal.
Which is my way, being man.
Gods may stay in mid-heaven, the Son of Man
    has climbed to the Whitsun zenith,
But I, Matthew, being a man
Am a traveller back and forth
So be it."

                    D. H. Lawrence, "St. Matthew,"
                    (from The Evangelistic Beasts*)*

After he failed to complete the complex "In the Direction of the Beginning" and "An Adventure from
a Work in Progress" (published in 1938 and 1939)
Thomas suddenly turned to an unadorned "straight"
prose style. Where the poetry written after 1940 re-
tained the symbolic richness of the early style tem-
pered by increased clarity of theme and delivery,
the later prose shed the symbolic landscape entirely.
1939, notes Vernon Watkins, was "the year in which
he abandoned the struggling, symbol-charged prose
of the intensely subjective early stories and began
to write stories about human beings living and be-
having exactly as they used to live and behave when
he was a child."[1] Thomas, who was penniless, job-
less, and about to become a father, was impelled by
a motivation as realistic as his new style: "I've been
busy," he wrote to Watkins, "over stories, pot-boiling

149

stories for a book, semi-autobiographical, to be finished by Christmas."[2] When *Portrait of the Artist
as a Young Dog* was about to be published he com-
mented: "I've kept the flippant title for—as the pub-
lishers advised—moneymaking reasons."[3] Thomas
seems to have guessed rightly that the British public, which was beginning to have its fill of adult violence in real life, would welcome stories of a
Swansea and Carmarthen childhood.

I

As if the tumultuous psychic drama of the early
prose had become too intense to be borne, Thomas
deliberately turned away from strictly inward concerns to confront the events of the social world. In
"The Peaches," written in 1938, his autobiographical
hero is frightened by being left outside a country
bar at night. As he huddles outside, he remembers a fantasy invented in the safety of his Swansea
home. This "story" contains a number of elements
from the early prose: made up in "the warm, safe
island of my bed, with a sleepy midnight Swansea
flowing and rolling round outside the house," it involved a demon who clung to his hair bat-like as he
"battled up and down Wales after a tall, wise,
golden, royal girl from Swansea Convent" who
"vanished like the grass-green of the cart that was
a dark, grey mountain now standing between the
passage walls" (*Portrait*, pp. 10–11).[4] When the
bar door swings open to emit a dazzling light the
boy is mercifully rescued from the world of fantasy

and brought into a world where he is much more interested in becoming "aware of me myself in the exact middle of a living story." By the second tale in the series the young hero has so successfully banished the dream-world of the early tales that he joins the posse of barber, tailor, and butcher in rescuing his grandfather from an imaginary journey into death.

The theme of initiation into the mysteries of love, madness, and death is the same as in the early tales, but where Thomas had been involved in the struggles of his hero he now creates a boyhood mask through which he can observe others. In "The Peaches," "Patricia, Edith and Arnold," "Extraordinary Little Cough," "Just Like Little Dogs," "Who Do You Wish Was With Us?" and "A Visit to Granpa's," it is a social goal—a tea party, marriage, love affair, or proper burial—which is sought and lost. Taken as a series, the tales form a litany of what a boy might call "facing the facts." As the little balloon of hope pops at each denouement the hero is initiated into a new aspect of adult life.

Thomas' ability to choose the exactly appropriate detail or adjective serves him well in his new style. His account of Ann Jones' parlour in "The Peaches" is, in its biting particularity, a model of realistic description. The personality of Annie, as of Amabel Owen, is embodied in her household effects; but where Thomas shows Amabel's sinister nature bursting out of the house into a union with the demonic cycles he describes Annie's homely universe simply for itself.

The strikingly new style of *Portrait* undoubtedly owes something to James Joyce's *Dubliners*. In each of Joyce's tales there is a rising and falling of hope for some experience which will transform the doldrum of Irish dailiness into enchantment. The boy in "Araby" (which resembles "After the Fair" in setting), in "The Sisters," and in "An Encounter" is being initiated into death, disillusionment, and perversion in a manner strikingly similar to that of Thomas' autobiographical hero. The failed romance of "Eveline" and "Two Gallants" resembles the breaking up of "Patricia, Edith and Arnold;" "After the Race" can be compared, in the hero's quest for social communion through drunkenness, to "Old Garbo;" while "A Mother," "A Little Cloud," "A Painful Case," and "Ivy Day in the Committee Room" deal with the same kind of tawdry middle-class tragedy as "Just Like Little Dogs" and "Where Tawe Flows." Both *Dubliners* and Thomas' *Portrait* form a series of stories grouped according to different phases of growing up. Thomas, however, never emerges from adolescent themes, and there is nothing comparable to "The Dead" or "Grace" in his collection.

The difference between Thomas' later prose and Joyce's early prose is again one of dramatic perspective. In his short stories Joyce achieves the distance from his heroes that he insisted upon in his *Portrait of the Artist as a Young Man*: the reader shares the shattered expectations of the protagonist without regard for the narrator. Thomas' readers are more apt to identify with him, witnessing other people's tragedies through a combination of his experience and his hero's innocence. As a result Joyce's often acrid tone is replaced with a whimsical melancholy, as of experience seen through the eyes of innocence. As Thomas' series draws to an end, however, the innocent boy is replaced by a hero who is just beginning to suffer his own disappointments. Although in "Just Like Little Dogs" the narrator flees back to his boyhood room from the tangled lives of the lovers, in "Old Garbo" he is moved from detachment to empathy through the medium of alcohol. In the last and finest of the stories Thomas' autobiographical detachment gives way to complete sympathy with the hero, who in his tragic disappointment in love is akin to Joyce's Gabriel.

Thomas was periodically afflicted—as the Poetry Notebooks suggest—with the kind of depression that one is able to glimpse in "One Warm Saturday," although in a 1946 broadcast he was to look back upon a seaside holiday with affectionate recollection.[5] As he sits in the midst of the gay beach crowd, the hero is moved "to an old shame and pity; outside all holiday, like a man doomed forever to the company of his maggots" (*Portrait*, p. 136). He meets a young girl "at the gates of the Gardens" who beckons and calls his name "over the bushy walls." Although he longs for her companionship, he is bitterly distrustful of his own worthiness: "If Venus came in on a plate," he says to himself, "I would ask for vinegar to put on her." Once more we have Thomas portraying Marlais' desire for an orchard maiden, and once more a hero feels com-

pelled to kiss the scarecrow sisters. As if to repudi-
ate this lapse back to the early prose world of Eve
and Lilith, Thomas quickly asserts that the hero has
"no need of the dark interior world when Tawe
pressed in upon him and the eccentric ordinary people came bursting and crawling . . . out of the common, wild intelligence of the town" (*Portrait*, p. 143).
"One Warm Saturday" is an appropriate conclusion
to the series of initiatory glimpses into adulthood of
which Thomas' *Portrait* is composed. As the story
progresses he abrogates his detached point of view
to proclaim his allegiance to the "small and hardly
known and never-to-be-forgotten people of the dirty
town [who] had lived and loved and died and, always, lost" (*Portrait*, p. 160).

The unfinished "Adventures in the Skin Trade" of
1941 deals with a young man similarly determined
to participate in the "real life" of "real people."
Where in "The Orchards," "The Visitor," and (impli-
citly) in "The Enemies" and "The Holy Six" the
heroes had moved away from the dwelling places of
men into the country of the unconscious, in "Adventures" the city is the source of experience. From the
time of his earliest visits Thomas both desired and
feared London, and in the later prose it came to re-
place the arbitrary sea-goddess as a source of love
and death and a place of ambition and failure. "I've
just come back from three dark days in London,
city of the restless dead," he wrote in 1938. "It really is an insane city, & filled with terror . . . its glam-
our smells of goat."[6] Later he was to recall his
early visits, when he roomed with Alfred Janes and

Mervyn Levy, as a golden time of fellowship and unrealized potentiality.[7] He continued to sway between desire for the city's adventures and fear of its talons until his death in what for him was the most fascinating and terrible of all cities.

In "Prologue to an Adventure" Thomas attributes the infernal aura of harlots and temptation to the city. His hero, under the influence of rural Protestant moralism, sees it as a place of sin where "the last tide-spinning of the full circle" of apocalypse is taking place. With its "seven deadly seas" and "seven gutters" it is, indeed, a kind of upside-down celestial city. Like the boy of the *Portrait* tales the young hero is insulated from the shocks of the environment, still watched over by the "golden sexless women" who bore him in purity at the beginning of the world. Much of the tale is written in the style of the early prose, although the devil's minion of the 1930–1932 and 1933 Notebooks, as well as the poet-hero of the early prose, has been transformed through nostalgia into a cherub of light.

In "Adventures in the Skin Trade," which Thomas began in 1941, good and evil have ceased to motivate his autobiographical hero who, as a preliminary to submitting himself to London as a tabula rasa, systematically destroys the effects of his suburban parlour. Thomas presents the snug objects of the boy's house with a realistic care which aptly conveys their tawdriness: he tears a photograph of his mother—with her "pastelled silk scarf, the round metal badge of Mrs. Rosser's Society, and the grandmother's cameo brooch on the vee of the knitted jumper"—into pieces until "the whole of her dead, comfortable face remained on one piece, and he tore it across the cheeks, up through the chins, and into the eyes" (*AST*, p. 11).[8] The motive behind the boy's destructiveness is his desire to present himself without "home or help" to a London which he presumes will introduce him to new dimensions of human experience.

Samuel's adventures, ironically, are not into sexual initiation but back into infancy: sister, mother and father are replaced by Polly, Mrs. Dacey ("He's only a baby") and Allingham, while Allingham's roomful of furniture takes the place of the cluttered suburban parlour. The bottle in which Samuel's finger is stuck is as much a pun on his being "stuck on his bottle" as a phallic symbol, while the tepid bathwater and rubber duck which are the setting of his seduction suggest amniotic rather than seminal fluids. The comic Freudian and surrealist puns are the most successful aspect of the tale, which Thomas intended as a series of "adventures" in which the hero's "skins" would be stripped off one by one like a snake's until he was left in a kind of quintessential nakedness to face the world.[9] His projected conclusion involved Samuel being arrested stark naked in Paddington Station. It was possibly because the tale was turning out regressive rather than progressive, a parody on the quest for initiation which was the serious theme of the early tales and of *Portrait*, that Thomas finally abandoned it. "My prosebook's going well, but I dislike it," he wrote in May 1941; "It's the only really dashed-off piece of work I re-

member doing . . . it's indecent and trivial, sometimes funny, sometimes mawkish, and always badly
written which I do not mind so much."[10] It was
probably because of this genuine dislike of the style
that Thomas was unable to finish the novel.

The early prose had been built out of the inner
vision of an extraordinarily subjective young man.
Conceived during the time of his first loves and pub-
lications, it depended upon an alternate idealization
and terror of woman and upon a quest for poetic
inspiration. Into it, as into the early poetry, were
woven the symbols and themes of all of the readings with which he had crammed himself from an
early age. The later prose, pared of symbolism and
mythology, diverges from both the earlier and later
poetry as well as from the early prose. As it evolved
it came more and more to represent a desire for objectivity in dramatic presentation which Thomas was
never to achieve.

In a 1946 broadcast Thomas declared that "as Mr.
de la Mare went on writing, his children went on
growing. They did not grow into youths, but into
children."[11] Where in "Adventures in the Skin
Trade" Samuel Bennet sheds his childhood skins
only to find that the city is even more puerile, the
characters of *Under Milk Wood* exist wholly apart
from the world in the fancied innocence of adult
children. Invented first as an "insane area" to be
ironically contrasted to a "sane" world (as "The
Town Was Mad") Llaregubb evolved into a wholly
self-contained Eden, innocent of conflict and tension. The final form was conceived in 1945 as

"Quite Early One Morning" and was completed during the bitterest period of Thomas' life. He intended it as "an entertainment out of the darkness" of a time when only brief periods of lucidity marked the process of alcoholic debilitation. It is thus, like Blake's *Songs of Innocence*, a recollection of innocence through the eyes of experience. From it Thomas purged all darkness, suffering and, indeed, dramatic tension: as T. H. Jones has aptly noted, it should be considered as a "piece" and not as a play at all.

Under Milk Wood is unique among all of Thomas' work in its total reliance upon the verbal richness of imagery and the rhythm of language in the absence of any narrative line or thematic conflict. It is unfortunately better known than many of his more representative works: it should be understood as an incidental idyll belonging to a period of Thomas' life when the lyric force which had run richly and fully through the early prose was to produce, in conjunction with a mature mastery of the narrative mode, the excellent lyric narratives of his later years.

II

By 1940 Thomas was trying to express themes that were too broad for the shorter lyric with its narrative line concealed beneath a "host of images." When he turned after 1940 to such straightforward themes as the birth of a son and air raids, and when he resurrected such earlier, topical pieces as "The Hunchback in the Park" (1932, 1941) and "After the

funeral" (1933, 1938) many critics and readers an-
nounced his "maturity." At the same time, however,
that he seemed to have abandoned the subjective,
inward world of the early prose, he was beginning
to revive its heroes, adventures, and mythological
structure within the sustained, formal boundaries of
the longer narrative poems.

In a synopsis of the "Ballad of the Long-legged
Bait" Thomas said that it was about "a young man"
who "goes fishing for sexual experience" only to
catch "the church and the village green."[12]   As in
the earlier tales, the flood motif has both sexual and
mythological significance, the fisherman-hero being
analogous to Jessie Weston's fisher-king and to Edward Davies' Dylan ail Mor.[13]   At the outset the girl
represents the instinctual life of a sadistic or at least
destructively moralistic fisher: "Oh all the wanting
flesh his enemy / Thrown to the sea in the shell of
a girl."   For the first thirty verses it seems as if she
were being torn apart by the whales, sea horses,
angel fish and rainbow fish who "bend in her joys"
in "huge weddings in the waves."   It becomes clear
towards the middle of the ballad, however, that—as
in "The Enemies," "The Holy Six," "The Visitor,"
"The School for Witches," and the two fragments—
the narrative is cyclical.   New birth spins out of
degeneration and a Blakean regeneration out of the
battle of the sexes: "The centuries throw back their
hair / And the old men sing from newborn lips" in
the renewal of the land out of the flood.

The girl, like the children who in "My world is
pyramid" become entangled in shells, accretes all

sorts of solid substances until she rises out of the sea as a new land:

Insects and valleys hold her thighs hard,
Time and places grip her breast bone,
She is breaking with seasons and clouds.
                    (*CP*, p. 174)[14]

Once more the unconscious sea is buried beneath the earth until "nothing remains / Of the pacing, famous sea but its speech." The hero is left stranded on dry land, lost and alone in the churches and towns of conscious, social existence. The exuberant pursuit of the girl gives way to a stationary, fixed existence, while the cockle boat is replaced by "home." The narrative line describes the same personal evolution as such earlier lyrics as "When once the twilight locks," but it is made more compelling and coherent by the use of a more fully dramatic hero and heroine. For the first time the "out of the sea" imagery of such a poem as "When once the twilight locks," the battle with the woman of the poems finished for *The Map of Love* and *Twenty-Five Poems*, and the narrative style perfected in the early prose are blended with a mature lyric craftsmanship into a new and highly successful genre.

The narrative poems of the later years are widely spaced among Thomas' shorter lyrics, each one a lengthy, complex piece involving immense correction and revision. "Vision and Prayer," which was finished in August of 1944, was probably begun (as Dr. Maud tells us) to commemorate Aeronwy's birth the year before. The most personal of the narrative

poems, it contains the fullest and most coherent development of Thomas' religion, as we saw in Chapter 3. In "A Winter's Tale," which he finished in
late 1944 or early 1945, the "certain promise" of the
early prose was fulfilled. The landscape combined
the island-and-flood setting of "The Map of Love"
with the farm-in-the-valley structure of "The Tree,"
"The Enemies," "The Holy Six," and "The Dress":

> It is a winter tale
> That the snow blind twilight ferries over the lakes
> And floating fields from the farm in the cup of the vales.
> (*CP*, p. 131)

The "snow blind twilight" which pervades the poem
characterizes a surreal world where no grass grows
beneath the snow, perhaps the zone between life
and death explored by Peter and the Reverend
Davies. The imagery, endowed with solidity and
radiance, is no more ephemeral than that of the
Jarvis world of the early prose. The language of
"A Winter's Tale" resembles that of *Under Milk
Wood* where "each cobble, donkey, goose and goose-
berry street is a thoroughfare of dusk, and dusk and
ceremonial dust, and night's first darkening snow,
and the sleep of birds."[15] Like many of the early
prose tales the action of *Under Milk Wood* circles
around a focal point where the protagonists achieve
their individual consummations: "In the warm
White Book of Llareggub," Thomas assures us, "you
will find the little maps of the islands of their contentment."[16] The hero and heroine of "A Winter's
Tale" are not the realistically described "Mog" and

"Myfanwy" of the play but quintessential lovers seeking an embrace that is more mystical than earthly. As in "The Burning Baby," the countryside undergoes a metaphorical transformation, the snow to "drifting bread" and in its dazzling brightness to the immortal fire of the sun.

The hero brings together in his quest several of the early adventures. Like the hero of "The Mouse and the Woman" he dwells alone and seeks a mate "who is not human." Like Marlais and the madman of "The Dress" he must run through the country towards "the always desiring centre of the white / Inhuman cradle and the bride bed forever sought" (*CP*, p. 133). Just as the madman, Marlais, and Peter achieve a poetic inspiration inseparable from mortal destruction, so here the hero's quest consummates in an agon: "he prayed to come to the last harm / And the home of prayers and fires." In the dance that accompanies the rising of the she-bird at the middle of the poem, a number of mythological sources mentioned in Chapters 2 through 4 coalesce. The sacred horses of the British, "centaur dead" or as extinct as centaurs, rise to "turn and tread the drenched white / Paddocks"; the druid runes and leaf-symbols are present where "The carved limbs in the rock / Leap, as to trumpets" and "Calligraphy of the old / Leaves is dancing." All of this occurs in "the poles of the year," probably the two equinoctial Alban-festivals. The she-bird herself, in her fusion of snow, fire, and woman, could be a description of Awen, the bardic muse whose birds sang at the creation of the world.

The woman whom the hero seeks is thus—like Amabel Owen, the sisters in "The Orchards," the heroines of the two fragments, and the Medusa of "Altarwise by owl-light"—a fusion of beauty and terror. The images of fluidity, corporeality, fire, and breath, the four bardic elements, play in and out of the poem until they merge in an apotheosis of bird and man. The denouement, where the hero is engulfed in the wings of the omnipotent she-bird, is delivered with a lyric mastery that marks the poem as one of Thomas' crowning achievements.

Although "A Winter's Tale" was Thomas' last fully developed narrative lyric, he planned a complex epic poem to be entitled "In Country Heaven." In a B. B. C. broadcast on September 25, 1950, as part of the projected epic he read three poems: "Over Sir John's hill," "In country sleep," and "In the white giant's thigh." Although the three lyrics have been taken as Thomas' farewell to his own life, he meant them as part of an elegy for the death of the entire earth. "In Country Heaven" was so Blakean in conception that Thomas prophesied the kind of criticism for it that Blake still receives for his *Prophetic Books*: "the plan of it is grand and simple and . . . the grandeur will seem, to many, to be purple and grandiose and the simplicity crude and sentimental."[17]

The three poems were to be set on a cosmic scale, with the creator weeping over the death of the earth and the heavens darkened by his sorrow. The "Countrymen of heaven," whose prototypes wept and sang in Blake's "Milton" and "Jerusalem," sit under the hedges in the dark to sing, Thomas says, of "what they remember, what they sense in the sub-merged wilderness and on the exposed hair's breadth of the mind, what they feel trembling on the nerves of a nerve, what they know in their Edenic hearts, of that self-called place" ("Three Poems," p. 157). Thomas may have had the same Blakean frame-work in mind when he composed *Under Milk Wood*, where he took the point of view of a fond and some-times ironic narrator looking down upon the foibles and aspirations of an engagingly childish people.

The narrator of the three poems is Thomas-as-a-countryman-of-heaven who remembers the earth as it lay awaiting destruction. In "Over Sir John's hill" he thinks of the pathos of innocent birds who must be killed, although they are presently oblivious of the "hawk on fire" hanging over them "in a hoisted cloud" of a gallows. This "fiery tyburn" is, by anal-ogy to Hopkins' windhover, a deadly Christ, the fig-ure of death and judgment of the last day. He is also a bomb, with a "viperish fuse" hanging under his wing (probably *the* bomb, as the atomic bomb was thought of after 1945). Among all of the silly birds, "green chickens of the bay," the heron (which in Welsh mythology is a symbol of priest and fisher-king) alone has sense enough to grieve with the countryman.

Where in "Over Sir John's hill" Thomas mourns with the hapless victims of apocalypse, he takes a less sombre point of view in "In the white giant's thigh." Here he grieves not like a creator for his falling sparrows nor, as in "In country sleep," like a father for his daughter, but like a randy Zeus who has loved women as he found them all over the earth. Devoted to all shapes and sorts of women, the poem is a raucous "Legend of Good Women" which could be entitled "The Lovesong of Great-Uncle Jarvis." In this elegy to the joys of sexual intercourse Thomas carries out with considerable success the complex intention of "Into her Lying Down Head."

It is the earlier "In country sleep," however, which marks Thomas' fullest incorporation of the problems of the early prose into his narrative lyrics. Here the role of the pathetic birds of "Over Sir John's hill" is played by a young girl over whose innocence the narrator watches and broods. On one level the theme is of puberty—how the virginity of the young daughter is to be protected against the inevitable thief of innocence. The Thief, while bringing experience with its knowledge of death, is also Christ, since the young girl seems to represent the virgin earth violated by incarnation. Just as in "Vision and Prayer" Thomas here would have man bounded by the "known dark" country of the personality, only to realize that incarnation and sexual initiation are analogous stages in historical and personal development. Here, as in Yeats' "Crazy Jane talks to the Bishop," the created earth proclaims the fact that "Nothing can be sole or whole / That has not been rent."

At the outset Thomas-as-narrator is determined that the girl remain in deepest sleep, innocent of all of the "hearthstone tales" with which even green innocence abounds. "Never fear or believe," he warns, the tales of princes and wolves, of sexual initiation and the "broomed witch's spume" of darker rites. Nothing, he insists, "skulks in the dell but moonshine echoing clear." As if warning his daughter and himself away from those glens where he, like Machen, may have become convinced of the supernatural, he cautions her away from the fables which serve as a bridge to experience, the dark stories which brace youth for confronting life and death.

Thomas' desire (which he also expressed through the young hero of "One Warm Saturday") is impossible, for "out of the beaked, web dark and the pouncing boughs / Be you sure that the Thief will seek a way sly and sure." The transcendent deity will find a way for his incarnation no matter what barriers are put up, a shattering entry which Thomas mourns here, as in "Vision and Prayer," as an inexorable part of human existence. The world of fable and fantasy is terrible for both its destruction and its wonder, for even as he warns the girl he himself bursts out with irrepressible joy at the marriage of spirit and matter. As in "A Prospect of the Sea" "A hill touches an angel!" for

> Now the tales praise
> The star rise at pasture and nightlong the fables graze
> On the lords'-table of the bowing grass.
>
> (*CP*, p. 182)

The natural world is possessed by the supernatural: the rooks are "cawing from their black bethels" and the sap in the branches changes into "the pastoral beat of blood through the laced leaves." As in "Vision and Prayer" divinity incorporates itself into the "thisness" or "inscape" of created things, in spite of the poet's desire for the less complex comforts of a world that is the "heart's size."

III

"In country sleep" unites the themes of many of the earlier narrative tales and shorter poems in a summary of Thomas' understanding of the human saga. It is impossible for any human being to remain in the "slow deep sleep" of wholly instinctual or unconscious life, an Eden which must be shattered by the advent of consciousness. The first expression of the awakening intellect is fable, a mode of initiation into sexual and human experience. Thomas' tales tell both of princely lovers and Red Riding-hood wolves, of golden maidens and Medusa-hags, since the end of every quest for life must be an affirmation of both its destructive and creative potentialities. Like the heroes of the early prose tales the heroine of "In country sleep" must confront a vision that is not unitive but contrary, expressive of the cyclical alternation of object and subject, love and hate. Written near the end of Thomas' creative life, the poem reasserts the importance of the narrative element in human experience. In it the metaphorical transformations that characterized the early prose sweep once more over the landscape to affirm the worth of Thomas' lifetime epic of tales and fables, "The Saga from mermen / To seraphim," the tension between myth and religion which had occupied him from his earliest writings.

The use of unconscious materials in literature, as we have seen in the quick fading of surrealist writings, cannot in itself qualify a work as art or determine its stylistic success. Myth, dream, and madness are exceedingly raw materials which do not constitute literature unless endowed with exceptional shape and form. Thomas' quests for woman and for poetic inspiration had to be transmuted through narrative structure, rhetorical facility, and a gift for imagery before they could stand on their own as a successful art form. As I have demonstrated in Chapter 1, each of Thomas' narratives is made up of a series of forward thrusts on the part of the hero, shaped into an orderly progression of events which often suggests the stateliness of a ritual dance. In and out of this adventure are woven patterns of conflicting imagery, springing from the landscape over which the hero moves and from similar quests in analogous mythology.

In the early prose, as in the later narrative poetry, there is a particularly felicitous blending of personal material, thematic imagery, and a mythological narrative. As a result it is not only a unique genre among Thomas' prose and poetry but also provides, in its clear juxtaposition of narrative line and a "host of images," a perspective for the study of the narrative and lyric modes in the rest of his works. From the vantage point of our understanding of the early prose it is possible to elucidate the latent narrative line of the poetry that both preceded and accompanied it in composition. It also is possible to determine a clear evolution in style and delivery towards the final narrative lyrics. Indeed, such poems as "Author's Prologue," "Poem on his Birthday," and especially "In country sleep" seem to turn back towards the early prose fables to give to Thomas' total work the same self-regenerating cyclical structure that characterizes each individual piece.

Appendixes
Notes
Bibliography
Index

A Comparative Chronology
of the Prose and Poetry

Although it is difficult to determine exactly when Thomas worked on a given piece, the dates in the Red Notebook manuscript of the early prose and the dates of composition of the first complete versions of the poetry provide a general comparative chronology of composition which should help to orient the critic in the relationship between the prose and the poetry.

Wherever possible, I have listed items under the date of composition, indicating whether later versions were written. Until December of 1934 the dates refer to the Red Notebook or to one of the Poetry Notebooks, as indicated. Titles followed by "(Maud)" bear the composition dates provided by Ralph Maud in his "Chronology of Composition," Appendix I to *Entrances to Dylan Thomas' Poetry*. Although all of Thomas' works of fiction are listed, the poetry is listed selectively: the purpose of this chronology is not bibliographical but comparative.

KEY

RN   the Red Notebook
N   with date, a Poetry Notebook
PHJ   Pamela Hansford Johnson, Lady Snow
VW   the late Vernon Watkins, in letters to the author or in Dylan Thomas' *Letters to Vernon Watkins*
Maud Professor Ralph N. Maud
(   )   indicate unpublished works

THE PROSE	THE POETRY
	1930, December ("Today, this hour I breathe." 1930–1932 N)—an early version of "Today, this insect"
	1931, September ("Why is the blood red and the grass green." 1930–1932 N)
	c. 1932, July–1933, January "Do you not father me" (Maud)
1932, November "Uncommon Genesis" ("The Mouse and the Woman"?) PHJ[1]	
	1933, February ("Had she not loved me at the beginning." Feb. 1933 N)
	1933, April "And death shall have no dominion" (Feb. 1933 N) "Not from this anger" (Feb. 1933 N) ("First there was the lamb on knocking knees." Feb. 1933 N) —later incorporated in "Altarwise by owl-light"

1. Ralph Maud, letter of March 30, 1963 to the author.

THE PROSE	THE POETRY
	("Within his head revolved a little world." Feb. 1933 N)

THE POETRY

("Within his head re-
volved a little world."
Feb. 1933 N)

1933, May
("Before we sinned."
Feb. 1933 N)—later
"Incarnate devil"
("No man believes."
Feb. 1933 N)

1933, July
"Why east wind chills"
(Feb. 1933 N)
"Ears in the turrets hear"
(Feb. 1933 N)
("A woman wails her
dead among the trees."
Feb. 1933 N)

1933, August
"Shall gods be said to
thump the clouds"
(Feb. 1933 N)
"Grief thief of time,"
stanza I (Aug.
1933 N)
("Shiloh's seed." Aug.
1933 N)

1933, September
("Take the needles and
the knives." Aug.
1933 N)
("Not forever shall the
lord of the red hail."
Aug. 1933 N)
"Before I knocked"

THE PROSE	THE POETRY
	(Aug. 1933 N) "In the beginning" (Aug. 1933 N)
	1933, October ("The eye of sleep." Aug. 1933 N) — later "I fellowed sleep" "The force that through" (Aug. 1933 N)
1933, November "After the Fair" (RN)	1933, November "When once the twilight locks no longer" (Aug. 1933 N) "Light breaks where no sun shines" (Aug. 1933 N)
1933, December "The Tree" (RN)	1933, December "This bread I break" (Aug. 1933 N)
1934, January "Martha" ("The True Story") RN	
1934, February "The Enemies" (RN)	1934, February "A process in the weather of the heart" (Aug. 1933 N) "Foster the light" (Aug. 1933 N)
1934, March "The Dress" (RN)	1934, March ("The shades of girls." Aug. 1933 N) — "Our eunuch dreams"

THE PROSE	THE POETRY
1934, April "The Visitor" (RN)	1934, April "I see the boys of summer" (Aug. 1933 N) "If I were tickled by the rub of love" (Aug. 1933 N)
1934, May Thomas was at work on a *Doom on the Sun* draft. PHJ[2]	c. 1934, May "I dreamed my genesis"[3]
1934, July "The Vest" (RN)	c. 1934, July "All all and all the dry worlds lever" (Maud)
1934, August ("Gaspar, Melchior, Balthasar." RN)	c. 1934, August "My world is pyramid" (Maud)
1934, September "The Burning Baby" (RN)	c. 1934, September "When, like a running grave" (Maud)
1934, October "Anagram," first version of "The Orchards" (RN)	
1934: Listed but not included in RN "The Holy Six"[4]	

2. Letter of April 7, 1963 to the author gives permission to cite this fact, previously conveyed by PHJ to Ralph Maud.

3. From Ralph Maud, "Chronology of Composition" in *Entrances to Dylan Thomas' Poetry* (Pittsburgh, 1963), henceforth cited as (Maud).

4. This note is in pencil and may have been added later.

THE PROSE	THE POETRY

"The Map of Love"
"The Witch" ("The
  School for Witches"?)
"Uncommon Genesis"
"The Manor"[5]
"The Diarists"[4]
"The Knife"[5]
"At the End of the
  River" ("The End of
  the River," published
  Nov. 1934 in *New
  English Weekly*)
"The Tramp"[5]
"The Enemies United"
"Selmer"[5]

1934–1935: Typed by PHJ
    and her mother
  "The Horse's Ha"
  "The Mouse and the
    Woman" (story be-
    ginning "In the eaves
    of the lunatic
    asylum' "—PHJ)

1934, December–1935,
    March
  "I, in my intricate
    image"
  and revisions of
  "My hero bares his
    nerves"
  "In the beginning"
  "I fellowed sleep"
    (Maud)

c. 1935 (VW[6]):
  "A Prospect of the Sea"
  "The Lemon"
  Work on "The Or-
    chards" (VW, after-
    word to *AST*)

1935, April–May
  "Hold hard, these
    ancient minutes in the
    cuckoo's month"
    (Maud)

---

4. This note is in pencil and may have been added later.

5. No known version extant.

6. Dylan Thomas, *Letters to Vernon Watkins* (London, 1957),
pp. 14–15.

THE PROSE	THE POETRY
	1935, Summer Sonnets I–VII of "Altar-wise by owl-light" (Maud)
	1935, October "How soon the servant sun" (published— Maud)
	1935, December–1936, February Sonnets VIII–X of "Altarwise by owl-light" (Maud) "It is the sinner's dust-tongued bell" (Maud) A number of revisions, including "Today, this insect"
1937, Summer Publication of "Prologue to an Adventure"	
	1937, November "I make this in a war-ring absence" (Maud)
1938 "The Peaches"	
1938, March Publication of "In the Direction of the Beginning"	1938, March "How shall my animal" (Maud)

THE PROSE	THE POETRY
"A Visit to Granpa's"[7]	
1938, July "One Warm Saturday"	
	1938, October "A saint about to fall" (Maud) "Twenty-four Years" (Maud)
	1938, December "Once it was the colour of saying" (Maud)
	1939, January "Because the pleasure-bird whistles" (Maud)
1939, March Publication of "An Adventure from a Work in Progress"	1939, March "If my head hurt a hair's foot" (Maud)
1939, May Publication of "The True Story"	1939, May "When I woke" (Maud) "Unluckily for a Death" (Maud)
1939, July Publication of "Old Garbo"	
1939, August Publication of *The Map of Love*	

7. "These stories probably written immediately prior to publication . . . " Maud.

THE PROSE	THE POETRY
(*The World I Breathe*, the American edition, came out in 1940)[8]	
1939, September Publication of "Extraordinary Little Cough"	
1939, October Publication of "Just Like Little Dogs"	
1939, December Publication of "The Fight" "Patricia, Edith, and Arnold" "Where Tawe Flows" "Who Do You Wish Was With Us?"	
1940, April Publication of *Portrait of the Artist as a Young Dog*[9]	

8. *The Map of Love* included "The Enemies," "The Tree," "The Visitor," "The Orchards," "The Mouse and the Woman," "The Map of Love," and "The Dress." To these were added in *The World I Breathe* "The Burning Baby," "A Prospect of the Sea," "The Holy Six," and "Prologue to an Adventure."

9. *Portrait* included "A Visit to Granpa's," "One Warm Saturday," "The Peaches," "Old Garbo," "Extraordinary Little Cough," "Just Like Little Dogs," "The Fight," "Patricia, Edith, and Arnold," "Where Tawe Flows," and "Who Do You Wish Was With Us?"

THE PROSE	THE POETRY
	1940–1941 "Ballad of the Long- legged Bait" (Maud) "Into her Lying Down Head" (Maud)
1941, May–June "Adventures in the Skin Trade"	
	1941, July "Among those Killed in a Dawn Raid" (Maud)
	1943–1944 "Vision and Prayer"
	1944 "Ceremony after a Fire Raid" "Poem in October"
	1945 "A Refusal to Mourn" "A Winter's Tale" "Fern Hill"
	1945–1951 Composition of "Do Not Go Gentle"
	1946–1947 "In country sleep"
	1949 "Over Sir John's hill"
	1949–1951 Composition of "Poem on his Birth- day"

THE PROSE	THE POETRY
	1950 "In the white giant's thigh"
	c. 1951, July–August "Lament" (all from Maud)
1952, October Publication of "The Followers"	
	1952 November "Author's Prologue" Publication of *Collected Poems*
1953 First reading of *Under Milk Wood*	
1955 Posthumous publication of *A Prospect of the Sea* *Adventures in the Skin Trade and Other Stories*[10]	

10. *A Prospect of the Sea* included the title story, "The Lemon," "After the Fair," "The Visitor," "The Enemies," "The Tree," "The Map of Love," "The Mouse and the Woman," "The Dress," "The Orchards," and "In the Direction of the Beginning." To these were added in *Adventures in the Skin Trade* the title story and "An Adventure from a Work in Progress," "The Horse's Ha," "The Vest," "The True Story," "The Followers," "The School for Witches," "The Holy Six," "The Burning Baby," and "Prologue to an Adventure."

The Critics and the Problem of Influence

Two careful studies of Dylan Thomas' work, one conceived before his death, have been devoted to external influences suggested by internal or textual evidence, and it is no coincidence that both attempt to elucidate the symbolically esoteric sonnets of the "Altarwise by owl-light" sequence. Elder Olson's *The Poetry of Dylan Thomas*—published in 1954 but partially composed in 1948—contains one of the earliest recognitions that since Thomas' works are mutually referential in their various symbols, images, and mytho-narrative structures they should be considered as parts of a "symbolic universe." (William T. Moynihan, in his recent *The Craft and Art of Dylan Thomas*, reaches a similar conclusion in a chapter on the poet's "Total Vision.") Olson describes three predominant types of symbolism in Thomas' early work: natural (water and dryness, light and dark); conventional (belonging to such systems of symbolic conception as astronomy, physics, the occult, religion); and personal (such as Thomas' frequent use of wax to suggest death, or oil to suggest life). This type of codification is similar to the incidental analogies mentioned by Tindall (see above, p. 35) and to the categorical approach to Thomas' "world" upon which Clark Emery's *The World of Dylan Thomas* is organized. Olson describes Thomas' symbolic universe as "myth" not merely in the sense that myth is "often regarded as evidence merely of the superstitious or naively imaginative tendencies of the ancients" but as part of a "symbolic formulation of knowledge, scientific or otherwise."[1]

1. Elder Olson, *The Poetry of Dylan Thomas* (Chicago, 1961), p. 67.

A good deal has been said about the "primitive" nature of Thomas' inspiration, as if his poems had sprung from his soul in as "natural" a way as do chants from the lips of an aborigine. Thomas' contact with such boosters of a literary "psycho-myth" as Eugene Jolas and the *transition* contributors has been overlooked, probably out of critical embarrassment at appearing "academic" in treating Thomas' earthy poems. It should be remembered that "myth" is a term used only by postprimitive, self-conscious mythologizers, and that when Thomas calls a hero a "folkman" he betrays his literary distance from the "folk." In the literature of the nineteenth and twentieth centuries, myth is often a self-conscious mode of composition in which individual images, symbols, and other motifs are worked into narrative tale or "adventure" or into implicit "narrative line" of a lyric poem. To extend Olson's categories, modern "myths" are sometimes natural or primitive (as in tales centering upon the sun as hero or god, the sea as mother or death); sometimes part natural and part conventional (as in the sun-hero–Hercules analogy or, as in "Vision and Prayer," the sun-son pun); and sometimes personal (as in Thomas' use of the sun and dry land to represent reason and society as contrasted to the amniotic, unconscious, and creative sea). Quite often in modern poetry, as Olson implies and Thomas' work illustrates, these and several other levels interact in a given work.[2]

Olson bases his interpretation of the sonnets largely upon parallels between their intrinsic symbolic constructs and Flammarion's *The Wonders of the Heavens*, a popular work on astrology which he assumes that Thomas may have read. "The real point here," he ex-

2. Olson lists six levels of analogy as important to the understanding of Thomas' sonnets, here abbreviated: 1) the parallel between man's life and the seasons; 2) between the sun and man; 3) a level of private symbolism; 4) between sun-heroes and Greek mythology (Hercules); 5) between the constellation Hercules in astrology; and 6) a Christian interpretation of 4 and 5. Ibid., p. 64.

plains, "is not the historic fact but the possibility that the poet may have known and used the tradition."[3] The burden of proof of Olson's assumption rests upon its textual applicability: his position seems to be that whether or not Thomas actually read Flammarion, there are textual evidences that astrological patterns of some sort help to elucidate the sonnets. "What Thomas wanted," he notes, "was for the reader to begin with the idea that he *might* be speaking literally; to declare something a symbol or a metaphor only after it was evident that it could not be a literal expression; to find out, in that case, what kind of a symbol or metaphor it was; and so go eventually, *from the text*, to Thomas' meaning."[4] The assumption seems to be that any symbol or metaphor is by necessity a reference to a system of meaning outside of the given text. Olson thus places considerable emphasis on the conventional references of symbolism, and his contribution to Thomas scholarship consists in his willingness to assume the astrological hypothesis and let the burden of proof rest upon its application to the text. It should be noted, then, that although Olson stresses the symbolism of the constellation Hercules Thomas mentions that hero nowhere in the sonnets. "Whatever stand we may take on the significance of myth," declares Olson, "there is no doubt whatsoever that the pagans associated certain constellations with Gods, demigods, and heroes."[5] The question left dangling is, did Thomas?

In a more recent study of "Altarwise by owl-light" entitled *The Religious Sonnets of Dylan Thomas*, H. H. Kleinman works himself into a position similar to Olson's. Dylan Thomas was not a Welsh bard, he asserts, nor a surrealist, (nor—one reads between the lines in

3. Olson, *The Poetry of Dylan Thomas*, p. 65 *n.* 4.
4. Ibid., p. 62.
5. Ibid., p. 65.

spite of his respect for Olson—an astrologer) but a mystic. "I believe the sonnets are a deeply moving statement of religious perplexity concluding in spiritual certainty," he declares, and goes on to describe their locus as "in a passion play, [where] innocence and religiosity, awe and familiarity, devotion and ribaldry are curiously mixed." Here Kleinman is in good company: Olson had declared the ultimate level of the sonnets to be a reworking of Greek and astrological material according to Christian convictions; Aneiran Talfan Davies moves in *Dylan: Druid of the Broken Body* toward an assessment of Thomas' proximity to orthodox Christian dogma; and Jacob Korg devotes an excellent opening chapter of his *Dylan Thomas* to Thomas' "Rhetoric of Mysticism." Certainly there is more Christian terminology than Greek in the sonnets, but Kleinman's references to external sources are often more interesting than elucidating. Take, for example, his explanation of the lines from Sonnet I:

Old cock from nowheres and the heaven's egg
With bones unbuttoned to the half-way winds,
Hatched from a windy salvage on one leg.

"The image is drawn," he explains, "from a legend about a cock which began crowing 'Christus natus est' at the moment of nativity."[6] He gives as a source a ballad of St. Stephen and Herod from Child's *English and Scottish Popular Ballads*, thus providing a religious or Medieval-mystical flavor to his explication. He seems here to be veering aside from the point, affixing a source to the image derived from a legend with which he, but not necessarily Thomas, is familiar. He would be more properly advised, I would think, to mention Horatio's account of the "bird of dawning" which "singeth all

6. H. H. Kleinman, *The Religious Sonnets of Dylan Thomas* (Berkeley, Calif., 1963), p. 21.

night long" in *Hamlet*, since we know from FitzGibbon that Dylan Thomas was imbued with Shakespeare from an early age.

This instance might be taken as quibbling on my part were the technique of affixing his own predilections to a given image not prevalent in Kleinman's study—a technique which becomes ludicrous when he states that the "heaven's egg" derives from "a reference to one of many autogenetic myths of God creating himself out of an egg" and accompanies the statement by a footnote to "a similar concept of Ovigenesis found in Pseudo-Clementine literature of the Ante-Nicene fathers." "Hatched from a windy salvage" is annotated similarly with a reference to the "choral ode of cosmogony from the *Birds* of Aristophanes."[7] Certainly "heaven's egg" seems to refer to a suprapersonal conception, but are we not much closer to elucidation if we remember the world egg or "Mundane Shell" hatched in Blake's *Prophetic Books*, which we can say with more certainty were available to the poet? Kleinman, as Aneiran Davies, seems concerned with providing links between a form of orthodox religion-mythology and Thomas' personal symbolic system. In his *Dylan Thomas* Jacob Korg also notes a mixture of the worldly and the profane in Thomas' symbolism, and attributes it to a "secular mysticism." "What is called mysticism in literature," he notes, "has as its subject a mixed cosmos, a point of intersection between natural and supernatural orders . . . the secular mystic must use language in ways that forestall a banal intelligibility and force the mind towards new ranges of meaning."[8]

We are left with the problem of finding the biographical origins of the "secular mystic" paradox: can it be attributed to the clash of a primitive, romantic personality

7. Ibid., p. 113 *n.* 13.
8. Jacob Korg, *Dylan Thomas* (New York, 1965), p. 28.

with non-conformist religion, or does the "point of intersection" derive from some less obvious paradox in historic Welsh religion? Thomas' religious and cultural
background in Wales, as has been pointed out most recently and cogently by FitzGibbon and by Ackerman, is
definitive to the understanding of his personal vision.
"General cultural movements such as surrealism and
Freudian theories of art," notes Ackerman, "had, at best,
clinical rather than religious or moral pretensions. It
was his Welsh environment which offered a background
of thought and culture fostering belief in the more primitive, mystical, and romantic conception of the poet."[9]

If, as nearly everyone asserts, Thomas is some sort of
religious poet, then we must consider in depth the kind
of religion prevalent in his environment; if he uses mythology in a "primitive" fashion we must certainly ascer-
tain the nature of any pseudo-primitive mythologizing
with which he or his father might have been familiar.
FitzGibbon deals thoroughly with the religious background of key members of Thomas' family, and his
material about Great-Uncle Gwilym Marles, the Unitarian preacher-poet, casts interesting light upon the convictions (or lack of them) of Dylan Thomas and his
father. I have carried the implications of nineteenth-
century "immanentism" a few steps further in Chapter
3 ("Religion in the Early Prose").

As for the Welsh background, both FitzGibbon and
Ackerman treat it as a technical influence: FitzGibbon
provides a fascinating analysis of the effect of Welsh
language and rhetoric upon the first generation of non-
Welsh–speaking writers, and Ackerman concentrates
upon the influence of "bardic" technique upon Thomas'
craft.[10] Little has been done, however, to evaluate the

9. John Ackerman, *Dylan Thomas, His Life and Work* (New
York, 1964), p. 5.
10. Constantine FitzGibbon, *The Life of Dylan Thomas* (Bos-

parallels between Thomas' uniquely personal religion and Welsh immanentism or to assess the influence of the purportedly "historic" druid mythology and theology upon Thomas' symbolic universe.

---

ton, 1965), pp. 4–9. John Ackerman, "The Welsh Background," in C. B. Cox, ed. *Dylan Thomas* (Englewood Cliffs, N. J., 1966), pp. 25–44. See also Ackerman, *Dylan Thomas,* p. 29.

Some Notes on the Contents
of transition, 1929–1936

The essays, manifestos, stories, and poems in this avant-garde periodical of 1927–1938 bear striking analogy to the concerns underlying Dylan Thomas' early prose. I have reproduced here a partial list of these materials for the interest of Dylan Thomas' readers, who will also find further analogies in the notes to Chapter 5.

I. *transition* no. 18, November 1929
This issue contains a lengthy section entitled "The Synthetist Universe, Dreams and the Chthonian Mind."

A. Jolas, in "Notes on Reality" (pp. 15–20), says that "In examining this region [of the dream], the psychology of depth has facilitated the comprehension for the processes of creation. The old dogmas of critical dictators are automatically thrown overboard. We now have come near knowing the sources of inspiration, and the secret of genius is out."

B. Other writers list specific dreams. Then follow:

C. Critical analyses of Joyce

D. A section "On the Revolution of the Word," describing Joyce's efforts to recreate language itself

E. Joyce's "Work in Progress" (early drafts from *Finnegan's Wake*)

F. The following manifesto on p. 239:

> THE NOVEL IS DEAD   LONG LIVE THE NOVEL
>
> The novel as practiced today is an archaic form that no longer answers the needs of the modern psyche.
>
> It presents a rigid, exhausted formula, and has grown unwieldy as an instrument of expression.
>
> It lacks the possibility of further evolution, because it clings to the descriptive requisites of a banal universe.

It has grown artificial, and, like the rhyme, represents a straitjacket to the creative visionary of our age.

The novel of the future will take no cognizance of the laws imposed by professors of literature and critics.

The novel of the future will be a compendium of all the manifestations of life in a timeless and spaceless projection.

The novel of the future will use telegrams, letters, decrees, fairy tales, legends, and dreams as documents for the new mythos.

The novel of the future will be a plastic encyclopedia of the fusion of subjective and objective reality.

The novel of the future will synthesize all the styles of the epoch in an effort towards unity.

The novel of the future will plunge into the underworld of our being and create fables in consciousness.

The novel of the future will produce new myths of the dynamic movement of the century.

The novel of the future will express the magic reality in a language that is non-imitative and evolutionary.

[signed]
Harry Crosby
Stuart Gilbert
Eugene Jolas
Theo Rutra
Robert Sage

G. Narrative efforts, a number reminiscent (or prophetic of?) Dylan Thomas' early prose. Note particularly George Tichenor's "Summertime," concerning a suicide in industrial society which ends, "He felt a stroke in his stomach and heard something slap against the pavement. His last sensation was of a deadening pressure in his chest—a drumming noise—and dust—so much dust—he tried to close his swollen lips" (p. 278).

II. *transition* no. 19–20, June 1930
An ad on the front of no. 19–20 calls out, "We want myths and more myths" and announces "Young England in Revolt," giving the names of "j. bronowski, wm. emp-

son, hugh sykes, basil wright, john davenport, george reavy, william archer" and others. This number contains a long section on "Dream and Mythos."

A. C. G. Jung's "Psychology and Poetry" includes the statement: "The psychological novel, regarded as a completed whole, explains itself. It is, as it were, its own psychology, which the psychologist would at best have to complete or to criticize, but which does not answer the highly essential question, how this author came upon this novel" (p. 25). Jung goes on to distinguish between two sources of a work of art: a) the intentional source, springing from conscious motivation; and b) the source springing from the psychological [unconscious] apparatus itself. The first produces the psychological novel, the second the visionary novel. The second type should not be reduced to the first: "This type of work of art is not the only one that stems from the nocturnal sphere; seers and prophets, leaders and enlighteners also feed upon it." It is primitive, barbarian, dark.

> It is, therefore, entirely logical that the poet should return to the mythological figure (or at least to pseudohistory) in order to find a fitting expression for his experience. Nothing would be more erroneous than to assume that the poet creates from the material of tradition, he works rather from the primal experience, the dark nature of which requires mythological figures, and thus draws avidly to itself everything that is akin, to be used for self expression. . . . he also needs a refractory and contradictory form of expression to conjure the terrific paradoxicalness of this vision with approximate validity. (pp. 36–37; and see above, pp. 28, 35)

Jung goes on to distinguish between Freud's personally motivated man and his own view of the poet functioning as collective man. "For his life is, of necessity, full of conflicts, since two forces fight in him: the ordinary man with his justified claim for happiness, contentment and guarantees for living on the one hand, and the ruthless creative passion on the other which under certain conditions crushes all personal desires into the dust, on the other hand. Thus it is that the personal destiny of so many artists' lives is so extremely unsatisfactory, indeed, tragic" (p. 42; and see above, pp. 52–53).

B. Jung's entry is followed by selections entitled "Evolution of the Senses" and also "Cambridge Experiment, a Manifesto of Young England."

III. *transition* no. 21, March 1932
The preface to this March 1932 issue contains the following statement by Eugene Jolas: "In the face of a materialistic despotism which places the 'concept' before the living imagination, and the force of the will before that of life, in the face of a näive optimism of progress, in the face of machine-mammonism, we feel the necessity of a revolution of the soul" (p. 7).

A. No. 21's first section is entitled "Metanthropological Crisis," including an article by Leo Frobenius, whose graphs of the undersea journey of the soul are described by Jung in *Symbols of Transformation*. Here Frobenius locates two levels of life, the practical and the daily vs the "paideumatic and psychic currents" located in the depths of the ocean. "We shall find it (this rhythm, its chords and melodies) in the inter-play of the two great primal paideumas, which have risen since the two Ice Ages like a gigantic arc from the two pedestals which we today still call Orient and Occident, and which will prove to be Northland and Southland (North Europe and Africa)" (p. 116, an extract from Frobenius, a lecture given before the Institut für Kultur-morphologie, Frankfurt am Main).

B. Another section, entitled "Poetry is Vertical," follows; this includes some of Hölderlin's "Poems of Madness."

C. "The Mantic Personality" contains an article by Gottfried Benn, entitled "The Structure of the Personality." This involves: (1) an outline of the geology of the "I"; (2) the biological basis of personality described as "once thought cerebral, but now known to involve 'the whole organism'"; and (3) an explanation of his "geological principle," used to describe how "the pathological moods of the soul are the repetition of life on a lower scale of organic nature. . . . We carry the remnants and traces of former evolutionary stages in our organism, we observe how these traces are realized in the dream, in ecstasy and in certain conditions of the insane" (pp. 201–2). The personality "adjusts itself to the specific animal characteristic of each geological epoch: it is web-footed in the epoch of the victorious amphibiae, covered with hair during the ape period. It records all these changes: mentally, in the memory of mankind, as in the primal myths, the primal sagas, primal epics; and the body summarizes them in their rudiments, all these species of half-men and animal men, the species with scales and fish-bodies, the species with tails, with monkey coats, the giants, the chimeras" (p. 203).

IV. *transition* no. 22, February 1933

In his preface to this number, Jolas writes that "The Vertigral Age brings with it a recognition of the a-historic man, the religious man, the man who seeks a mystic union with the logos." Contents here include:

A. A continuation of Joyce's "Work in Progress," followed by "Marginalia to James Joyce's Work in Progess" in which Jolas asserts that "the principal criterion of genius is the capacity to construct a mythological world" (p. 101).

B. Stuart Gilbert, "Five years of *transition*." Gilbert writes: "Eugene Jolas was intimate with the leaders of the [surrealist] movement and it was this friendship with a severely exclusive group . . . that enabled him to publish a series of translations from their 'texts' in the early numbers of *transition*" (p. 141). This article is crucial to the study of the periodical.

V. *transition* no. 23, July 1935

In his preface here Jolas writes: "I suggest the paramyth as the successor to the form known heretofore as the short story or *nouvelle*. I conceive it as a kind of epic wonder tale giving an organic synthesis of the individual and universal unconscious, the dream, the daydream, the mystic vision. In its final form it might be a phantasmagoric mixture of the poem in prose, the popular tale of folklore, the psychograph, the essay, the myth, the saga, the humoresque" (p. 7). This volume contains:

A. An article entitled "Joyce and Mythology:
Mythology and Joyce," by Armand M. Petitjean.

B. A series of short statements by Goethe, Blake, and Nietzsche, on literature.

VI. *transition* no. 25, Fall 1936

The Fall 1936 number contains Dylan Thomas' "Then was my neophyte" (pp. 20–21) and "The Mouse and the Woman" (pp. 43–58). As is the case with nearly every issue, this one contains pictorial art, translations from various myths and fables of the world, and original "fables" in the manner of Jolas' paramyth.

Notes

INTRODUCTION: BIOGRAPHY AND THE
PROBLEM OF INFLUENCE

1. See E. W. Tedlock, ed., *Dylan Thomas: The Legend and the Poet* (London, 1960); John Malcolm Brinnin, *A Casebook on Dylan Thomas* (New York, 1960); and *Adam International Review*, Vol. 21, no. 238 (1953).

2. Aneiran Talfan Davies, "The Golden Echo" in *Dock Leaves*, Vol. 5 (Spring 1954), 10.

3. Caitlin Thomas, *Not Quite Posthumous Letter to my Daughter* (London, 1963), p. 27.

4. I am indebted to Mr. Leslie Rees of the Swansea Public Library for information about Thomas' family, and particularly for clippings from the *Swansea Grammar School Magazine*, Vol. 34 (March 1937), and *The Welshman* (December 26, 1952), on the retirement and death of D. J. Thomas, father of Dylan.

5. See Lita Hornick, "The Intricate Image: A Study of Dylan Thomas," unpubl. Ph.D. diss. (Columbia, 1958), pp. 27, 28, 39, 73, and 76.

6. The author has been informed by one academic researcher, X, that he went to London and Wales in the late fifties to interview Thomas' acquaintances. His source research had the following history:

X (*to Y, a close acquaintance of Dylan Thomas*): Do you think that Dylan could have read Y *Barddas* (*ab Ithel's compilation of druid lore*) or Edward Davies?

Y: Oh, yes, perhaps he might.

X (*in critical study*): Thomas read Y *Barddas*, and also Davies.

Y: (*on being checked by the author*): X certainly had an intelligent interest in the work, but I think perhaps he expected Dylan Thomas to be more interested in British druids than he was. If I said that he read Williams ab Ithel's translation of the *Barddas* or that he might have read it, it must have been only as a vague answer to a question about it from him, as I know nothing of this book, so certainly could not have mentioned it on my own. The same is true of Edward Davies' *Mythology and Rites*. I cannot really see Dylan Thomas reading such books, but of course he may have done. He really went back further, to the Garden of Eden, so please don't quote me in connection with books which I feel sure would only have been of marginal interest if he did read them.

7. Margaret Alice Murray, *The God of the Witches* (Essex, 1962), pp. 24, 77, 79. This work (first published in 1931) will be referred to in my text as "Murray."

8. Robert Graves, *The White Goddess* (New York, 1959), p. 445.

9. See Awstin et al., *The Religious Revival in Wales, 1904*, A *Western Mail* pamphlet collection of articles (London, 1904).

10. "The ideas of Darwin, Wallace, Spencer, Huxley, Taylor, Maclennon and Max Muller had been penetrating into Wales for some years before the revival and a crisis was facing non-conformity. The day schools, the country schools and the universities belonged to the New Knowledge, while the Sunday schools and the chapels belonged to the past. The most learned were leaving the church." Anonymous writer in *Cymru a'r Wydbodneth Newydd*, *Y Gehinen*, quoted in David Williams, *A History of Modern Wales* (London, 1950), p. 136.

11. Ibid, p. 250.

12. Joseph Campbell, *Occidental Mythology*, Vol. III in *The Masks of God* (New York, 1964), 464.

13. Aneiran Davies provides the data on W. Thomas' career in "The Golden Echo," p. 10 (see n. 2 above). I am indebted for information on Gwilym Marles to Glyn Jones, letter to the author of December 8, 1963. See also Constantine FitzGibbon, *The Life of Dylan Thomas* (New York, 1965), pp. 9–10.

14. A list of the authors of thrillers reviewed by Thomas for the *Morning Post* during 1935 includes M. G. Eberhart, Donald Macpherson, Jean Lilly, Robert Curtis, Dorothy Sayers, and Mary M. Atwater. See J. A. Rolph, *Dylan Thomas, a Bibliography* (New York, 1956), pp. 70–73.

15. Daniel Jones, memoir in Tedlock, ed., *Dylan Thomas*. Minor poets whose works Thomas reviewed in 1932 for the *Herald of Wales* were Walter Savage Landor, James Chapman Woods, H. A. W. Rott, Carl Morganwy, 'E. E.' of Caswell, Thomas Hood, Pierre Claire, and E. Howard Harris. Rolph, *Dylan Thomas, a Bibliography*, p. 69.

16. In *London Magazine*, Vol. 3 (September 1956), 14.

17. See William York Tindall, *A Reader's Guide to Dylan Thomas* (New York, 1962), p. 66.

18. Hornick, "The Intricate Image," p. 27.

19. Pamela Hansford Johnson, letter of July 4, 1963 to the author, stating that Thomas probably read the *Mabinogion*. This collection of Welsh tales has been translated by Gwyn and Thomas Jones (London, 1949).

20. "The real influences on Dylan's early stories, I would guess, are the work of Caradoc Evans, the stories of T. F. Powys, and perhaps French surrealist prose which he might have read in translation." Glyn Jones, letter of August 13, 1963 to the author.

21. See Arthur Machen, *The Hill of Dreams* in *The Complete Works* (London, 1923), pp. 160–61.

22. Arthur Machen, *Far Off Things* in *The Complete Works* (London, 1923), p. 15.

23. Ralph Maud, ed., *The Notebooks of Dylan Thomas* (New York, 1967); and Donald Tritschler, "The Stories in Dylan Thomas' Red Notebook," forthcoming in *The Journal of Modern Literature* (Philadelphia: Temple University).

24. "The core of his [Rimbaud's] being was purity and innocence, with a yearning for absolute perfection; his sensitiveness was now wounded by the ugliness he had encountered and he revolted against it . . . and sought relief in complete disgust." Enid Starkie, *Arthur Rimbaud* (New York, 1962), p. 15.

25. Derek Stanford, *Dylan Thomas* (New York, 1954), p. 19.

26. "He went down for a few weeks in August 1933—this is probably his first substantial visit. In *Adventures* he talks of a January 1933 visit (this is not likely—perhaps there was a January 1932 visit?). He was working for the *South Wales Daily Post* in the summer of 1931, but he *might* have taken a trip down with Fred Janes who was to begin at the Royal Academy in the fall. The visit on which he met PHJ was from 23 February–5 March 1934 (his second substantial visit to London?)." Ralph Maud, letter of April 23, 1963 to the author.

27. J. H. Martin, letter to the editor of the *London Times Literary Supplement* (March 19, 1964), p. 255.

28. Keidrych Rhys, letter to the editor, ibid. (March 26, 1964), p. 255.

29. Dylan Thomas, letter to Richard Church, in Constantine FitzGibbon, ed., *Selected Letters of Dylan Thomas* (New York, 1966), pp. 160–61.

30. I am indebted for this information to the George Reavey cor-

respondence at the Houghton Memorial Library, Harvard University.

31. Dylan Thomas, letter to Henry Treece, in FitzGibbon, ed., *Selected Letters of Dylan Thomas*, p. 200.

32. C. G. Jung, *Symbols of Transformation* (New York, 1956), p. 388.

33. Constantine FitzGibbon, *The Life of Dylan Thomas* (Boston, 1965), p. 94.

34. Ralph Maud, "Dylan Thomas' Collected Poems: Chronology of Composition," *PMLA* Vol. LXXVI (June, 1961), 292-97. See also Ralph Maud, *Entrances to Dylan Thomas' Poetry* (Pittsburgh, 1963), pp. 121–48 (hereafter cited and referred to in my text as *Entrances*).

35. Tritschler, "Stories in Dylan Thomas' Red Notebook." The Red Notebook is in the Dylan Thomas collection of the Lockwood Memorial Library at the State University of New York at Buffalo. It contains the original versions of "The Tree," "The True Story," "After the Fair," "The Enemies," "The Dress," "The Visitor," "The Vest," "Gaspar, Melchior, Balthasar," "The Burning Baby," and "The Orchards" ("Anagram" or "Mr. Tritas on the Roofs").

36. Jacob Korg, "The Short Stories of Dylan Thomas," *Perspective* Vol. 1 (Spring 1948), 186.

37. Kenneth Burke, *The Philosophy of Literary Form* (New York, 1957), p. 62.

38. Maud, *Entrances*, p. 49.

39. FitzGibbon, *The Life of Dylan Thomas*, p. 41.

40. Northrop Frye, *Anatomy of Criticism* (Princeton, 1957), p. 110.

41. Maud, *Entrances*, p. 83.

42. Ibid., p. 4

43. Ibid., p. 90.

44. Ibid., p. 89.

45. Winifred Nowottny, "There was a Saviour," in C. B. Cox, ed. *Dylan Thomas* (Englewood Cliffs, N. J., 1966), pp. 68, 70. See also *The Language Poets Use* (London, 1962, 1965).

46. Frederick Hoffman, *Freudianism and the Literary Mind* (New York, 1959), p. 12.

47. Ibid, pp. 128–30. The late Professor Hoffman, to whose teaching at the University of Wisconsin in 1958–1959 I am indebted, used approximately the same categories.

48. Frye, *Anatomy of Criticism*, p. 3.

CHAPTER I: THE STRUCTURE OF THE EARLY PROSE

1. Pamela Hansford Johnson, letter of July 4, 1963 to the author.

2. Vernon Watkins, letter of February 27, 1963 to the author.

3. *A Prospect of the Sea* was published by J. M. Dent & Sons in London (1955). The collection *Adventures in the Skin Trade and Other Stories* was published by New Directions in New York (1955). Quotations in this study are taken from the New American Library Signet reprint of *Adventures* (New York, 1961), which will be referred to in the text as *AST*. (The tales discussed in this chapter can be found in both editions.)

4. See Reviews of *AST* in *Commonweal*, Vol. 62 (January 10, 1955), 262; the *New Yorker*, Vol. 31 (June 11, 1955), 158; the *Saturday Review of Literature*, Vol. 38 (July 2, 1955), 18.

5. Davies Aberpennar, review of "The Visitor" in *Wales*, Vol. II, No. 2 (1939–1940), 308; and Kingsley Amis, review of *A Prospect of the Sea* in *Spectator* (August 12, 1955), p. 227. See also the *London Times Literary Supplement*, Vol. 796 (September 30, 1955), 569.

6. G. S. Fraser, "Dylan Thomas," Chapter 15 in *Vision and Rhetoric* (London, 1959), pp. 224–25. See also Henry Treece, *Dylan Thomas, "Dog among the Fairies"* (London, 1949), p. 128.

7. C. G. Jung, "Psychology and Poetry," *transition* no. 19–20, (June 1930), p. 42. See Appendix C.

8. Dylan Thomas, "Replies to an Enquiry" in John Malcolm Brinnin, *A Casebook on Dylan Thomas* (New York: Thomas E. Crowell Co., 1960), p. 102.

9. Jacob Korg, "The Short Stories of Dylan Thomas," *Perspective*, Vol. 1 (Spring 1948), 184.

10. William York Tindall, *The Literary Symbol* (Bloomington, Ind., 1955), p. 130.

11. Ralph Maud, *Entrances to Dylan Thomas' Poetry* (Pittsburgh, 1963), pp. 81–103 (hereafter cited as *Entrances*).

12. Northrop Frye, *Anatomy of Criticism* (Princeton, 1957), p. 106.

13. Suzanne Langer, *Philosophy in a New Key* (Cambridge, Mass., 1952), p. 141.

14. Korg, "Short Stories," p. 184.

15. Tindall, *The Literary Symbol*, pp. 60–62.

16. T. H. Jones describes Evans' style as "based on the rhythms and idioms of Welsh nonconformity, a virile, exuberant, non-con-

forming prose that has influenced almost every Anglo-Welsh writer, and not least Dylan Thomas." T. H. Jones, *Dylan Thomas* (New York, 1963), p. 44. In a letter to the author of August 13, 1963, Glyn Jones affirms Evans' influence on Thomas.

17. Caradoc Evans, *The Earth Gives All and Takes All* (London, 1947), p. 1.

18. Caradoc Evans, *Nothing to Pay* (London, 1930), p. 27.

19. T. F. Powys, *Mockery Gap* (New York, 1925), p. 37.

20. T. F. Powys, *The Two Thieves* (New York, 1932), quoted in H. Coombes, *T. F. Powys* (London, 1960), p. 34.

21. T. F. Powys, *God* (New York, 1932), p. 41.

22. Coombes, *T. F. Powys*, p. 28.

23. Interview with Harvey Breit in the *New York Times Book Review* (February 17, 1952), p. 17.

24. Anna Balakian, *The Literary Origins of Surrealism* (New York, 1947), p. 1.

25. Tindall, *The Literary Symbol*, pp. 64, 91.

26. Kenneth Burke, *The Philosophy of Literary Form* (New York, 1957), p. 9.

CHAPTER II: MYTHOLOGY IN THE EARLY PROSE

1. C. G. Jung, *transition* no. 19–20 (June 1930), p. 36.

2. See Joseph Campbell, "Great Rome" and "Europe Resurgent," Chapters 7 and 9 in *Occidental Mythology*, Vol. III in *The Masks of God* (New York, 1964). Sir James Frazer, *The Golden Bough* (New York, 1950).

3. Joseph Campbell, *Creative Mythology*, Vol. IV in *The Masks of God*, (New York, 1968), 6–8.

4. A. L. Owen, *The Famous Druids* (Oxford, 1962), p. 27.

5. Campbell, *Occidental Mythology*, pp. 40–41.

6. Quoted by Campbell from Caesar's *Gallic War*, 6: 13–18 in *Occidental Mythology*, pp. 293–96.

7. See Robert Graves, *The White Goddess*, (New York, 1959) p. 4.

8. Dylan Thomas, *Selected Letters of Dylan Thomas*, Constantine FitzGibbon, (New York, 1968), p. 48.

9. Ibid, p. 43.

10. Edward Davies, *The Mythology and Rites of the British Druids*, printed privately by Booth (London, 1809) and *Celtic Re-*

searches on the Origin, Traditions and Language of the Ancient Britons, privately printed by Booth (London, 1804). These two volumes will hereafter be cited and referred to in my text as *Mythology and Rites* and as *Celtic Researches.*

11. Roger Sherman Loomis, *Wales and the Arthurian Legend* (Cardiff, 1956), pp. 154–55.

12. Campbell, *Occidental Mythology,* p. 470.

13. Dylan Thomas, *Collected Poems,* (New York, 1957) (hereafter cited as *CP*). Quotations in the text are from this edition.

14. Marie Luzi, memoir in *Adam International Review,* Vol. 21, no. 238 (London, 1953), p. 25.

15. Davies, *Celtic Researches,* p. 157.

16. Suzanne Roussilatt, memoir in *Dylan Thomas: The Legend and the Poet,* ed. E. W. Tedlock (London, 1960), p. 6.

17. Constantine FitzGibbon, *The Life of Dylan Thomas* (Boston, 1965), p. 24. FitzGibbon notes that "D. J. cannot fail to have been reminded of the name Dylan in the year of his son's birth. In July of 1914 an opera was staged at Covent Garden with the title, *Dylan, Son of the Wave.*" Ibid., p. 25*n.*

18. Robert Graves, *The White Goddess* (New York, 1959), p. 92.

19. Joseph Campbell, *Primitive Mythology,* Vol. I in *The Masks of God* (New York, 1959), 299–354.

20. Davies, *Mythology and Rites,* p. 163.

21. Ibid., p. 154.

22. Dylan Thomas, *Adventures in the Skin Trade and Other Stories,* a new American Library Signet reprint (New York, 1961) of the New Directions edition (New York, 1955). Quotations in the text are from the Signet edition (hereafter cited as *AST*).

23. Davies, *Mythology and Rites,* p. 172.

24. FitzGibbon, *The Life of Dylan Thomas,* p. 31.

25. Dylan Thomas, letter to David Higham in FitzGibbon, ed., *Selected Letters,* p. 224.

26. Robert Graves and Raphael Patai, "Some Hebrew Myths and Legends," *Encounter* (February 1963), p. 9.

27. See Dylan Thomas, review of M. K. Gandhi's *Songs from Prison* in *Adelphi,* Vol. 9 (January 1935), 256.

28. "The Rig Veda," *The Sacred Books and Early Literature of the East,* ed. Charles F. Horne (New York and London, 1917) Vol. IX, 19.

29. Ibid, p. 46.

30. Graves, *The White Goddess*, p. 98.

31. Arthur Machen, *The Great God Pan* in *The Complete Works* (London, 1923), pp. 81–82. Thomas might have had in mind the element Manred, "the original form of all the materials" into which God breathed life in the bardic genesis (*Y Barddas*, Williams ab Ithel, ed. [London, 1862] p. 371; see below, Chapter 3, *n*. 4).

32. Kenneth Burke, *The Philosophy of Literary Form* (New York, 1957), p. 607.

33. Davies, *Celtic Researches*, p. 195.

34. Harold Bayley, *Archaic England* (London, 1920), p. 674. Apple, fig, and vine were sacred to Dionysus.

35. Graves, *The White Goddess*, p. 31.

36. Davies, *Celtic Researches*, p. 157.

37. Eugene Jolas, *transition* no. 23, (July 1935), p. 7.

CHAPTER III: RELIGION IN THE EARLY PROSE

1. W. S. Merwin, "The Religious Poet," in *Dylan Thomas: The Legend and the Poet*, ed. E. W. Tedlock (London, 1960) pp. 236–47; and Stuart Holroyd, *Emergence from Chaos* (Boston, 1957), p. 89.

2. William York Tindall, *A Reader's Guide to Dylan Thomas* (New York, 1962), p. 127. In another view: "at times Christ is used as a simile. . . . But then we have the reverse situation. Christ appears as Himself in some poems, and metaphors are then found for him." Ralph Maud, *Entrances*, p. 95.

3. See D. H. Lawrence, *Apocalypse* (New York, 1932), pp. 37–38.

4. *Y Barddas*, Williams ab Ithel, ed., for the Welsh MS Society (London, 1862). William F. Skene, in his introduction to *The Four Ancient Books of Wales* (Edinburgh, 1868), asserts that ab Ithel developed the theory of bardic institution, named himself "Iolo Morganwyg," and wrote the entire collection (Vol. I, 29). I will refer to the collection in my text as *Y Barddas*.

5. Joseph Campbell, *Occidental Mythology*, Vol. III in *The Masks of God* (New York, 1964), 264.

6. ab Ithel, *Y Barddas*, p. lxxxi.

7. On p. 47.

8. Entry of April 16–20, 1933, February 1933 Notebook. Note also "the fantastic circle of the sun," April 2, 1933 in February 1933

Notebook; "I eye the ring of earth, the airy circle," September 30, 1933 in August 1933 Notebook; "the plus of God / Hammered within the circling roads of fire," Oct. 4, 1933 in August 1933 Notebook.

9. Dylan Thomas, *Collected Poems* (New York, 1957) (hereafter cited as *CP*). Quotations in the text are from this edition.

10. Edward Davies, *The Mythology and Rites of the British Druids*, printed privately by Booth (London, 1809), pp. 10–11.

11. ab Ithel, *Y Barddas*, p. 209.

12. e.g., "The Battle of Godeau," *The Book of Taliesin*, VII in Skene, ed., *The Four Ancient Books of Wales*, 276–77.

13. On p. 78 of the New American Library Signet collection, *Adventures in the Skin Trade and Other Stories* (New York, 1961) (hereafter cited as *AST*). *Adventures in the Skin Trade and Other Stories* was first published by New Directions (New York, 1955). Quotations in the text are from the New American Library edition.

14. ab Ithel, *Y. Barddas*, p. 95.

15. Ibid, p. 227.

16. After poem of August 29, 1933: "Shiloh's Seed," in August 1933 Notebook (but with arrow pointing to "Before I knocked" on opposite page).

17. Glyn Jones believes that Thomas meant the Jarvis countryside as a version of the Holy Land: "In the same way, the landscape of the Jarvis hills, whose image occurs again and again in these early short stories, served as a symbol for the country of Galilee." "Welsh Voices in the Short Story," *Welsh Review*, Vol. VI, (Winter 1947), 298.

18. See *Adelphi* (October 1934).

19. Quoted in Harold Bayley, *Archaic England* (London, 1920), p. 665.

CHAPTER IV: BLAKE AND THE OCCULT IN THE EARLY PROSE

1. Charles Williams, *Witchcraft* (New York, 1960), p. 79.

2. Harold Fisch, *Jerusalem and Albion: The Hebraic Factor in Seventeenth Century Literature* (New York, 1964), p. 14.

3. Meyer Howard Abrams, *The Mirror and the Lamp* (New York: Norton, 1958), pp. 218–25.

4. William York Tindall, *Forces in Modern British Literature* (New York: Vintage Books, 1956), p. 164.

5. A. E. Waite, *The Holy Kabbalah* (New York, 1929), p. 348.

6. Entry of August 29, in August 1933 Notebook.

7. Ralph Maud, ed., *The Notebooks of Dylan Thomas* (New York, 1967), p. 322n.

8. The basic elements of the Kabbalistic system are outlined in Christian Ginsberg's *The Kabbalah* (London, 1925); Madame Blavatsky's *Isis Unveiled* (Covina, Calif.: Theosophical University Society, 1950), and A. E. Waite's *The Holy Kabbalah* (New Hyde Park, N. Y., 1929). See also H. H. Kleinman, *The Religious Sonnets of Dylan Thomas* (Berkeley, 1963), pp. 74-76.

9. Northrop Frye, *Feaful Symmetry, A Study of William Blake* (Boston, 1962), p. 125, reference to *Jerusalem*, p. 27.

10. William Blake, "The Marriage of Heaven and Hell," in *Blake's Poems and Prophecies* (London, 1954), p. 43. All quotations from Blake are from this J. M. Dent and Sons Edition.

11. Blake, "Milton," in *Blake's Poems and Prophecies*, pp. 140–41.

12. S. Foster Damon, *William Blake, His Philosophy and Symbols* (Boston, 1924), p. 102. According to Lita Hornick, Thomas read this work and also Percival's *Circle of Destiny*.

13. D. H. Lawrence, *Apocalypse* (New York, 1932), pp. 87–88.

14. Poem dated October 1931, in the 1930-1932 Notebook. Maud, ed., *The Notebooks of Dylan Thomas*, pp. 20–27, 147–48.

15. Williams, *Witchcraft*, p. 127.

16. According to Robert Graves, Anna is a Pelasgian goddess, sister of Belus, related to the Sumerian Ama, the "mother." "Elsewhere," writes Graves, "the pedigree of Prince Owen, son of Howel the Good, is traced back to . . . *Anna mater ejus.*" Thus we might see Amabel Owen as the amalgamation of Ama and Belus, beautiful mother of the Prince, a "black goddess" only according to the inverse judgement of the theologically orthodox. See *The White Goddess*, (New York, 1959), pp. 408–10.

17. From the New American Library Signet edition of *Adventures in the Skin Trade and Other Stories* (New York, 1961), reprinted from the New Directions edition (New York, 1955). Quotations in the text are from the Signet reprint of *Adventures in the Skin Trade* (hereafter cited as *AST*).

18. See Jacob Korg, "The Short Stories of Dylan Thomas," *Perspective*, Vol. I, (Spring 1948), 184–91.

19. In the first version of the tale, quoted by Thomas in a letter to Pamela Hansford Johnson, these are "Mr. Stope, Mr. Edgar, Mr.

Stull, Mr. Thade, and Mr. Strich"—spite, greed, lust, death, and Christ. Permission to quote letter of March 30, 1963 to Dr. Maud granted by Lady Snow. Thomas may have been trying to recall the deadly sins: pride, covetousness, lust, anger, gluttony, envy, and sloth.

20. Dylan Thomas, *Collected Poems* (New York, 1957) (hereafter cited as *CP*). Quotations in the text are from this edition.

21. Williams, *Witchcraft*, p. 35.

22. Taliesin, writes George Borrow, called the whole Saxon race a coiling serpent: "A serpent which coils / and with fury boils." *Wild Wales* (London: J. M. Dent, and Sons, 1910), p. 27.

23. Margaret Alice Murray, *The God of the Witches* (Essex, 1962), pp. 57–63.

24. Ibid., p. 54.

25. Entry of February 1, 1933 in February 1933 Notebook.

26. Murray, *The God of the Witches*, p. 24.

27. See Harold Bayley, "Scouring the White Horse," Chapter VIII in *Archaic England* (London, 1920).

28. Marjorie Adix, memoir in *Dylan Thomas: The Legend and the Poet*, ed. E. W. Tedlock (London, 1960), p. 66.

29. Glyn Jones, *Western Mail* (April 21, 1958).

30. See verse on p. 46 in the Red Notebook, entry of September 1934.

31. Murray, *The God of the Witches*, p. 96.

32. Quoted by Ralph Maud in *Notebooks*, p. 28.

33. Poem of May 23, 1933 in February 1933 Notebook.

34. Blake, "Jerusalem," in *Blake's Poems and Prophecies*, p. 171.

35. Thomas, *Collected Poems*, p. 47.

36. "Glad Day," property of the Philadelphia Art Museum. See Frye, *Fearful Symmetry*, p. 209.

37. Entry of September 13, 1933 in August 1933 Notebook.

38. Quoted by Geoffry Moore, in Tedlock, ed., *Dylan Thomas*, p. 251.

CHAPTER V: SURREALISM AS A LITERARY METHOD

1. John Bayley, *The Romantic Survival*, (London, 1957), p. 82.

2. Paul Charles Ray, "The Surrealist Movement in England," unpubl. Ph.D. diss. (Columbia, 1962), p. 52.

3. These "Notes" first appeared as "Poetic Manifesto" in the

Texas Quarterly, Vol. IV, (Winter 1961). They were reprinted as "Notes on the Art of Poetry" in *A Garland for Dylan Thomas*, George Firmage and Oscar Williams, eds. (New York, 1963).

4. George Reavey, notes to the Dylan Thomas letters, courtesy of the Houghton Memorial Library, Harvard University.

5. Sir Herbert Read, *Surrealism* (London, 1936), p. 76.

6. Dylan Thomas, *Adventures in the Skin Trade and Other Stories*, New American Library Signet reprint (New York, 1961) (hereafter cited as *AST*). Quotations in the text are from this edition. New Directions first published this collection in New York in 1955.

7. See also Richard Thoma, "Death Control," *transition*, no. 19–20 (June 1930), pp. 330–34.

8. Dylan Thomas, "Replies to an Enquiry," in John Malcolm Brinnin, *A Casebook on Dylan Thomas* (New York, 1960), p. 102.

9. Dylan Thomas, "Notes on the Art of Poetry," *A Garland for Dylan Thomas*, p. 152.

10. Jacob Korg, "The Short Stories of Dylan Thomas," *Perspective*, Vol. 1 (Spring 1948), p. 189.

11. Quoted in David Gascoyne, *A Short Survey of Surrealism* (London, 1935), pp. 63–67.

12. "The *latent* dream thoughts from the basic material for dream construction and exist in the unconscious in the form of wishes; they appear in the *manifest* dream (the dream we remember vaguely in the morning) in a variety of distorted forms." Frederick Hoffman, *Freudianism and the Literary Mind* (New York 1959), p. 11.

13. Kingsley Amis, "Thomas the Rhymer," *Spectator* (August 12, 1955), pp. 227–28.

14. Dylan Thomas, "The End of the River," in the *New English Weekly* (November 22, 1934), p. 134.

15. "Night through Night," *transition* no. 21 (March 1932), p. 174. See also Harry Crosby, "Dreams, 1928–29," *transition* no. 18 (November 1929), pp. 32–36; and Kathleen Connel, "The History of a Dream," *transition* no. 18 (November 1929), pp. 37–46.

16. Both included under "Four Primitive Documents," *transition* no. 23 (1934–1935), pp. 52–55.

17. By John Gogh, *transition* no. 21 (March 1932), pp. 48–57, an issue that also includes "Three Tales" by Franz Kafka.

18. Harry Crosby, *transition* no. 18 (November 1929), pp. 102–03.

19. Adalberto Varollanos, *transition* no. 18 (November 1929), pp. 278–83.

20. Poem dated April 16–20, 1933, in February 1933 Notebook.

21. Ray, "The Surrealist Movement in England," p. 259.

22. Very like such contributions to *transition* as Edward B. Mayer's "The Three Gloves," *transition* no. 18 (November 1929), pp. 59–63; George Tichenor's "Summertime," *transition* no. 18 (November 1929), pp. 279–83; and Georges Ribemont-Dessaignes' "The Eighth Day of the Week," *transition* no. 19–20 (June 1930), pp. 70–83.

23. Sir James Frazer, *The Golden Bough* (New York, 1950), p. 211. Thomas may have arrived at this symbol through association of Mousehole, Cornwall with the Freudian conversations of a lady whom he visited there. "My hostess . . . has unfortunately read too many books of psychology, and talks about my ego over breakfast," he bemoaned in a letter of April 20, 1936. *Letters to Vernon Watkins*, (London, 1957) p. 24.

24. Poem dated March 31, 1933, in February 1933 Notebook.

25. Ray, "The Surrealist Movement in England," p. 41.

26. "The fisherman lifts his net. It is a net that has no end. It is full of women, who are dripping wet, and who push each other about on the bank. The last one is Sadie. Frightened, the fisherman calls for help. Some passers-by spring forward behind her." *transition* no. 19–20 (June 1930), p. 77.

27. *The Doctor and the Devils* was published by New Directions (Norfolk, Conn., 1953), and *The Beach of Falesá* by Stein and Day (New York, 1963).

28. See above, *n.* 18 and *n.* 19. See also "Chainpoems" in *New Directions, 1940*, (Norfolk, Conn.: New Directions, 1940); and George Barker's "Elegies no. 1 and 2," Christopher Caudwell's "3 Poems," Bernard Guttridge's "Home Revisited," and Ruthven Todd's "Three Poems," in *New Verse*, Vol. 1 (January 1939).

29. See "Notes on the Art of Poetry," in *A Garland for Dylan Thomas*, p. 152.

CHAPTER VI: THE LATER PROSE AND NARRATIVE POETRY

1. Dylan Thomas, *Letters to Vernon Watkins* (London, 1957), p. 20.

2. Ibid., letter of August 25, 1939, p. 76.

3. Ibid., letter of January 30, 1940, p. 79.

4. Dylan Thomas, *Portrait of the Artist as a Young Dog* (New

York, 1940), and New Directions Paperbook no. 51 (1955) (hereafter cited as *Portrait*). Quotations in the text are from the Paperbook edition.

5. Dylan Thomas, "Holiday Memory," B. B. C. Welsh Home Service (October 25, 1946), in *Quite Early One Morning* (London, 1961), pp. 29–38.

6. Thomas, *Letters to Vernon Watkins*, p. 49.

7. Dylan Thomas, "A Painter's Studio," B. B. C. TV Broadcast (April 1953), in *Texas Quarterly* Vol. IV (Winter 1961).

8. The New American Library Signet reprint of the collection *Adventures in the Skin Trade and Other Stories* (New York, 1961), originally published by New Directions (New York, 1955).

9. See Vernon Watkins, "Afterword" to *Adventures in the Skin Trade* (New York, 1961), p. 188.

10. Thomas, *Letters to Vernon Watkins*, p. 102.

11. Dylan Thomas, "De la Mare as a Prose Writer" in *Quite Early One Morning* (London, 1954), p. 108.

12. William York Tindall, *A Reader's Guide to Dylan Thomas* (New York, 1962), p. 248.

13. According to Jessie L. Weston, Brons, the "rich fisher," caught a fish that fed all of his followers. She links it to the Salmon of wisdom," notable for its great fertility and for the fact that a taste of its flesh conferred all knowledge. See *From Ritual to Romance* (Garden City, N. J., 1957), Chapter IX, and pp. 116, 125–27, 135. See also above, p. 75.

14. Dylan Thomas, *Collected Poems* (New York, 1957) (hereafter cited as *CP*). Quotations in the text are from this edition.

15. Dylan Thomas, *Under Milk Wood* (New York, 1954), p. 84.

16. Ibid., p. 94.

17. Dylan Thomas, "Three Poems," B. B. C. broadcast September 25, 1950, published in *Quite Early One Morning* (London, 1961), p. 156.

Bibliography

ABBREVIATIONS

RN	The Red Notebook
AST	*Adventures in the Skin Trade*
PS	*A Prospect of the Sea*
ML	*The Map of Love*
WIB	*The World I Breathe*

I. WORKS BY DYLAN THOMAS*

Poetry Notebooks: 1930, 1930–32, February 1933, August 1933. Unpublished MSS, property of the Lockwood Memorial Library, State University of New York at Buffalo, Buffalo, New York.

The Red Notebook. December 28, 1933 – October 1934. Unpublished MS, property of the Lockwood Memorial Library, State University of New York at Buffalo, Buffalo, New York.

"After the Fair." RN, November 1933. *New English Weekly* (March 15, 1934). *ML, AST.*

"The Tree." RN, December 28, 1933. *Adelphi* (December 1934), *ML, AST, PS.*

18 Poems. London: The Sunday Referee and the Parton Bookshop, 1934.

"Martha" ("The True Story"). RN, January 22, 1934. *Yellow Jacket* (May 1939). *AST.*

"The Enemies." RN, February 11, 1934. *New Stories* (June–July 1934). *WIB, ML, PS, AST.*

"The Dress." RN, March 1934. *Comment* (January 4, 1936). *ML, WIB, PS, AST.*

"The Visitor." RN, April 1934. *Criterion* (January 1935). *ML, WIB, AST, PS.*

---

*Listed chronologically. The Notebook source with date of composition and the published source with its date are given. Collections in which the tales have been published follow, in abbreviated italics.

"The Vest." RN, July 20, 1934. *Yellow Jacket* (May 1939). *AST*.

"Gaspar, Melchior, Balthasar." RN, August 8, 1934.

"The Burning Baby." RN, 1934. *Contemporary Poetry and Prose* (September 1934). *WIB, AST*.

Reviews of *The Solitary Way* by William Soutar, *Squared Circle* by William Montgomerie, and *Thirty Pieces* by Sydney Salt. *Adelphi*, Vol. 8, (September 1934), pp. 418–420.

"Anagram" or "Mr. Tritas on the Roofs" ("The Orchards"). RN, October 1934. *Criterion* (1936). *ML, WIB, AST, PS*.

"Replies to an Enquiry." *New Verse*, no. 11 (October 1934), pp. 8–9; and in John Malcolm Brinnin, *A Casebook on Dylan Thomas*. New York: Thomas E. Crowell Co., 1960.

"The End of the River." *New English Weekly* (November 22, 1934), pp. 131–34.

Collected Poems, 1934–1952. London: J. M. Dent & Sons, 1952.

Review of *Songs from Prison* by M. K. Gandhi. *Adelphi*, Vol. 9 (January 1935), pp. 255-56.

"The Lemon." *Life and Letters Today* (Spring 1936). *PS, AST*.

"The Horse's Ha." *Janus* (May 1936). *AST*.

Letters to George Reavey, June 1936–January 1939. Annotated by Reavey. Unpublished letters, property of the Houghton Memorial Library, Harvard University, Cambridge, Mass.

"The School for Witches." *Contemporary Poetry and Prose* (August–September 1936). *AST*.

Twenty-Five Poems. London: J. M. Dent & Sons, 1936.

"The Mouse and the Woman." *transition* no. 25 (Fall 1936). *ML, WIB, PS, AST*.

"A Prospect of the Sea." *Life and Letters Today* (Spring 1937). *WIB, PS, AST*.

"The Holy Six." *Contemporary Poetry and Prose* (Spring 1937). *WIB, AST*.

"Prologue to an Adventure." *Wales* (Summer 1937). *WIB, AST*.

"The Map of Love." *Wales* (Autumn 1937). *ML, WIB, PS, AST*.

"In the Direction of the Beginning." *Wales* (March 1938). *AST*.

"An Adventure from a Work in Progress." *Seven* (Spring 1939). *AST*.

The Map of Love. London: J. M. Dent & Sons, 1939. The American edition was titled *The World I Breathe*. New York: New Directions, 1940.

Portrait of the Artist as a Young Dog. New York: New Directions, 1940. New Directions Paperbook no. 51. 1955.

Letters to Oscar Williams. August 5, 1942; May 13, 1952; November 22, 1952. Property of the Houghton Memorial Library, Harvard University, Cambridge, Mass.

Deaths and Entrances. London: J. M. Dent & Sons, 1946.

"Notes on the Art of Poetry." Summer 1951. In the *Texas Quarterly*, Vol. 4, (Winter 1951), pp. 44–53; and in Firmage, George and Williams, Oscar eds., *A Garland for Dylan Thomas*, pp. 147–152. New York: Clarke and Waye, 1963.

Interview with Harvey Breit. *New York Times Book Review* (February 17, 1952), p. 17.

In Country Sleep. New York: New Directions, 1952.

"I Am Going to Read Aloud." M.I.T. address March 7, 1952. *London Magazine*, Vol. 3, no. 9 (September 1956), pp. 13–17.

Llareggub. Botteghe Obscure IX (1952). *Under Milk Wood*. New York: New Directions, 1954.

"Adventures in the Skin Trade." Chapters I and II in *New World Writing*, nos. 2 and 3. New York: New American Library, (November 1952 and May 1953).

Collected Poems of Dylan Thomas. New York: New Directions, 1953, 1957.

"Seven Letters to Oscar Williams, 1945–53." *New World Writing*, no. 7. New York: New American Library (1955), pp. 128–140.

Letter of August 25, 1953 to Stephen Spender. Property of the Houghton Memorial Library, Harvard University, Cambridge, Mass.

Quite Early One Morning. Broadcasts February 15, 1943–March 30, 1954. London: J. M. Dent & Sons, (1954, 1961).

"An Artist's Studio." BBC broadcast, April 1953. The *Texas Quarterly* (Winter 1961), pp. 54–56.

Adventures in the Skin Trade and Other Stories. New York: New Directions, 1955; New American Library Signet reprint (1961).

A Prospect of the Sea and Other Stories and Prose Writings. Daniel Jones, ed. London: J. M. Dent & Sons (1955).

Letters to Vernon Watkins. April 1936–December 1952. London: Faber & Faber, 1957.

Selected Letters of Dylan Thomas. Constantine FitzGibbon, ed. New York: New Directions, 1966.

The Notebooks of Dylan Thomas. Ralph Maud, ed. New York: New Directions, 1967.

II. WORKS ON DYLAN THOMAS

Adam International Review. no. 238 (1953).

Ackerman, John. *Dylan Thomas, His Life and Work.* New York: Oxford University Press, 1964.

Amis, Kingsley. "Thomas the Rhymer." *Spectator* (August 12, 1955), p. 227.

AST reviews in the *Atlantic Monthly,* Vol. 38 (July 2, 1955), p. 81; the *London Times Literary Supplement,* no. 2796 (September 30, 1955), p. 569; the *New Yorker,* Vol. 31 (June 11, 1955), p. 138; the *Saturday Review of Literature,* Vol. 38 (July 2, 1955), p. 18; and *Time,* Vol. LXV (May 30, 1955), pp. 90–95.

Brinnin, John Malcolm. *A Casebook on Dylan Thomas.* New York: Thomas E. Crowell Co., 1960.

Brossard, Chandler. Review of AST in *Commonweal,* Vol. 62 (January 10, 1955), p. 161.

Cox, C. B., ed. *Dylan Thomas.* Englewood Cliffs, N. J.: Prentice-Hall, 1966.

Crampton, Michael. Review of AST in the *New Statesman,* Vol. L (September 10, 1955), pp. 305–6.

Davenport, John. "Dylan Thomas." *The Twentieth Century,* Vol. LLIV (December 1953), pp. 475–77.

Davies, Aneiran Talfan. *Dylan: Druid of the Broken Body.* London: J. M. Dent & Sons, 1964.

———. "The Golden Echo." *Dock Leaves,* Vol. 5 (Spring 1954), pp. 9–10.

Deutsch, Babette. "Alchemists of the Word." Chapter II in *Poetry in Our Time.* New York: Holt, 1952; rev. ed., 1956.

"Dylan Thomas: The Legend and the Puzzle." *London Times Literary Supplement,* no. 3236 (March 5, 1964), pp. 185–86.

Emery, Clark. *The World of Dylan Thomas.* Miami: University of Florida Press, 1962.

Firmage, George and Williams, Oscar, eds. *A Garland for Dylan Thomas.* New York: Clarke and Way, 1963.

Fraser, G. S. *Dylan Thomas.* London: The British Council, 1957.

FitzGibbon, Constantine. *The Life of Dylan Thomas.* New York: Atlantic-Little Brown, 1965.

———. Letter to the editor, *London Times Literary Supplement,* no. 3240 (April 2, 1964), p. 273.

Hawkins, Desmond. Review of *The Map of Love* in *Spectator,* no. 5800 (August 25, 1939), p. 300.

Holbrook, David. *Llareggub Revisited: Dylan Thomas and the State of Modern Poetry.* London: Bowes and Bowes, 1962; Urbana: University of Illinois Press, 1962.

Holroyd, Stuart. *Emergence from Chaos.* Boston: Houghton Mifflin, 1957.

Hornick, Lita. "The Intricate Image: A Study of Dylan Thomas." Unpublished Ph.D. dissertation, Columbia University, 1958.

Huff, William H. "Dylan Thomas: A Bibliography." Evanston: Reference Department of Northwestern University Library, 1953.

Jenkins, David Clay. "Dylan Thomas' *Under Milk Wood*: The American Element." *Trace,* Vol. 4 (Winter 1964), pp. 325–38.

Johnson, Pamela Hansford. Letters of March 13, 1963, and July 4, 1963 to the author.

Jones, Glyn. "Dylan Thomas and Welsh." *Dock Leaves,* Vol. 5 (Spring 1954), p. 24.

————. "Welsh Voices in the Short Story." *Welsh Review,* Vol. VI (Winter 1947), pp. 290–98.

————. Letters of August 13, 1963, November 8, 1963, and May 2, 1964 to the author.

Jones, Gwyn. "Welsh Dylan." *Adelphi,* Vol. 30 (First quarter 1954), pp. 109–17.

Jones, T. H. *Dylan Thomas.* Edinburgh: Oliver and Boyd, 1963; New York: The Grove Press Inc, 1963.

Kleinman, H. H. *The Religious Sonnets of Dylan Thomas.* Berkeley: University of California Press, 1963.

Korg, Jacob. *Dylan Thomas.* New York: Twayne, 1965.

————. "The Short Stories of Dylan Thomas." *Perspective,* Vol. 1 (Spring 1948), pp. 184–91.

Martin, J. H. Letter to the editor, *London Times Literary Supplement,* no. 3238 (March 19, 1964), p. 255.

Maud, Ralph N. "Dylan Thomas' Collected Poems: Chronology of Composition." *PMLA,* Vol. LXXVI (June 1961), pp. 292–97.

————. *Entrances to Dylan Thomas' Poetry.* Pittsburgh: University of Pittsburgh Press, 1963.

————. Letters of March 3, 1963, April 23, 1963, and March 19, 1964 to the author.

Meyerhoff, Hans. "The Violence of Dylan Thomas." *New Republic* (July 11, 1955), pp. 17–19.

Moynihan, William T. *The Craft and Art of Dylan Thomas.* Ithaca: Cornell University Press, 1966.

Olson, Elder. *The Poetry of Dylan Thomas.* Chicago: University of Chicago Press, 1954; rev. ed., 1961.

Poetry. Vol. LXXXVII (November 1955).

Rees, Leslie M. Letters of March 8, 1963 and May 1963 to the author.

Reifer, May. "Supernatural Stories of Dylan Thomas." Unpublished Master's essay, Columbia University, 1956.

Rhys, Keidrych. Letter to the editor, *London Times Literary Supplement*, no. 3239 (March 26, 1964), p. 102.

Rolph, J. Alexander. *Dylan Thomas: A Bibliography*. New York: New Directions, 1956.

Sennish, Robert Brady. "The Early Prose of Dylan Thomas." Columbia University. Master's essay, Columbia University, 1956.

Sitwell, Edith. "Four New Poets." *London Mercury*, Vol. XXXIII (February 1936), p. 386.

Stanford, Derek. *Dylan Thomas*. New York: Citadel Press, 1954.

Tedlock, E. W., ed. *Dylan Thomas: The Legend and the Poet*. London: Heinemann, 1960.

Tindall, William York. *A Reader's Guide to Dylan Thomas*. New York: The Noonday Press, 1962.

Treece, Henry. *Dylan Thomas*, "Dog Among the Fairies." London: Ernest Benn, 1949.

Tritschler, Donald. "The Stories in Dylan Thomas' Red Notebook." Forthcoming in *The Journal of Modern Literature*.

III. MISCELLANEOUS

ab Ithel, Williams, ed. *Y Barddas*. Published for the Welsh MS Society. London: Longman and Co., 1862.

Awstin et al. *The Religious Revival in Wales, 1904*. London: the *Western Mail*, 1904.

Balakian, Anna. *The Literary Origins of Surrealism*. New York: King's Crown Press, 1947.

Baring-Gould, S. *A Book of South Wales*. London: Methuen and Co., 1905.

Bayley, Harold. *Archaic England*. London: Chapman and Hall, 1920.

Bayley, John. *The Romantic Survival, A Study in Poetic Evolution*. London: Constable, 1957.

Blake, William. *Blake's Poems and Prophecies*. London: J. M. Dent & Sons, 1954.

Budge, E. A. Wallis, ed. and trans. *The Book of the Dead*. London: Kegan Paul, Trench, Trübner & Co., 1909.

Burke, Kenneth. *The Philosophy of Literary Form.* Baton Rouge: Louisiana State University Press, 1941. New York: Vintage Books, 1957.

——. "Surrealism." *New Directions,* 1940; Norfolk: The New American Library, 1940.

Campbell, Joseph. *The Masks of God.* 4 vols.: *Primitive Mythology, Oriental Mythology, Occidental Mythology, Creative Mythology.* New York: Viking Press, 1952–1968.

Coombes, H. *T. F. Powys.* London: Barns & Radcliff, 1960.

Damon, S. Foster. *William Blake, His Philosophy and Symbols.* Boston: Houghton Mifflin, 1924.

Davies, Edward. *Celtic Researches on the Origin, Traditions and Language of the Ancient Britons.* London: private printing, 1804.

——. *The Mythology and Rites of the British Druids.* London: private printing, 1809.

de la Mare, Walter. *Behold this Dreamer.* New York: Alfred Knopf, 1935.

Evans, Caradoc. *The Earth Gives All and Takes All.* London: Andrew Dakers, Ltd., 1947.

——. *Nothing to Pay.* London: Faber and Faber, 1930.

Fisch, Harold. *Jerusalem and Albion: The Hebraic Factor in Seventeenth Century Literature.* New York: Schoken Books, 1964.

Fraser, G. S. *Vision and Rhetoric: Studies in Modern Poetry.* London: Faber and Faber, 1959.

Frazer, Sir James. *The Golden Bough.* New York: Macmillan Co., 1950.

Frye, Northrop. *Anatomy of Criticism.* Princeton: Princeton University Press, 1957.

——. *Fearful Symmetry. A Study of William Blake.* Boston: Beacon Press, 1962.

Gascoyne, David. *A Short Survey of Surrealism.* London: Cobden-Sanderson, 1935.

Ginsberg, Christian. *The Kabbalah.* London: Longmans Green and Co, 1864; George Routledge and Sons, 1925, 1955.

Graves, Robert. *The Meaning of Dreams.* London: Cecil Palmer, 1924.

——. *The White Goddess.* New York: Creative Age Press, 1948; Vintage Books, 1959.

Hays, H. R. "The Surrealist Influence in Contemporary Poetry." *Poetry,* Vol. LIV (July 1939), pp. 206–9.

218 : BIBLIOGRAPHY

Hoffman, Frederick. *Freudianism and the Literary Mind.* New York: Grove Press, 1959.

Horne, Charles F., ed. *The Sacred Books and Early Literature of the East.* Vol. IX. New York and London: Parke, Austin, and Lipscomb, 1917.

Jones, Gwyn and Jones, Thomas, trans. *Mabinogion.* London: J. M. Dent & Sons, 1949.

Jung, C. G. "On the Relation of Analytical Psychology to Poetic Art." In *Contributions to Analytical Psychology,* edited by H. G. Baynes and F. Cary. London: Routledge & Kegan Paul, 1928.

——. "Psychology and Poetry." *transition* no. 19–20 (June 1930), pp. 25–42.

——. *Symbols of Transformation.* New York: Pantheon Books, 1956.

Kermode, John Frank. *Romantic Image.* London: Routledge and Paul, 1957.

Langer, Suzanne. *Philosophy in a New Key.* Cambridge, Mass.: Harvard University Press, 1952.

Lawrence, D. H. *Apocalypse.* New York: Viking Press, 1932.

Loomis, R. S. *Wales and the Arthurian Legend.* Cardiff: University of Wales Press, 1956.

Machen, Arthur. *The Complete Works.* Carleton Edition. London: Martin Secker, 1923.

Murray, Henry A., ed. *Myths and Mythmaking.* New York: George Braziller, 1960.

Murray, Margaret Alice. *The God of the Witches.* Essex: The Daimon Press, 1962.

North, F. J. *Sunken Cities: Some Legends of the Coast and Lakes of Wales.* Cardiff: University of Wales Press, 1957.

Powys, T. F. *The House with the Echo.* London: Chatto & Windus, 1928.

——. *God.* New York: Knopf, 1932.

——. *Mockery Gap.* New York: Knopf, 1925.

Ray, Paul Charles. "The Surrealist Movement in England." Unpublished Ph.D. dissertation, Columbia University, 1962.

Read, Sir Herbert. *A Concise History of Modern Painting.* New York: Praeger, 1959.

——. *Surrealism.* London: Faber and Faber, 1936.

Sergeant, Philip W. *Witches and Warlocks.* London: Hutchins & Co., 1936.

Skene, William F., ed. *The Four Ancient Books of Wales*. Edinburgh: Edmonston & Douglas, 1968.

Thomas, Caitlin. *Not Quite Posthumous Letter to My Daughter*. London: Putnam, 1963.

Tindall, William York. *The Literary Symbol*. Bloomington: Indiana University Press, 1955.

transition. no. 18 (Fall 1929), no. 19–20 (June 1930), no. 21 (March 1932), no. 22 (February 1933), no. 23 (July 1935), no. 24 (June 1936).

Waite, A. E. *The Holy Kabbalah*. New Hyde Park, N. Y.: University Books, 1929.

Weston, Jessie L. *From Ritual to Romance*. Garden City: Doubleday and Co., 1957.

Williams, C. R. "The Welsh Religious Revival, 1904–5." *British Journal of Sociology*, Vol. 3 (September 1952), pp. 242–59.

Williams, Charles. *Witchcraft*. London: Faber and Faber, 1941. New York: Meriden Books, 1960.

Williams, David. *A History of Modern Wales*. London: Penguin Books, 1950.

ab Ithel, Williams, 6, 27, 86–89, 92–93, 97. *See also* Religion, bardic

Ackerman, John, 189

"Adventure from a Work in Progress, An," 35, 36, 72, 74–76, 78, 94, 95, 116, 117, 120, 131, 149, 180

"Adventures in the Skin Trade," 32, 154–57, 182

Adventures in the Skin Trade and Other Stories, 20, 32, 183

"After the Fair," 142, 176

"After the funeral," 159

"All all and all the dry worlds lever," 92, 118, 177

"Alterwise by owl-light," 19, 22, 79, 90, 98, 117, 163, 173, 179

"Anagram." *See* "Orchards, The"

Apocalypse, 16, 35, 40, 85–86, 94, 104, 109–10, 111, 113, 127–28

"At the End of the River," 138, 178

"Author's Prologue," 75, 78, 169, 183

"Ballad of the Long-legged Bait," 20, 65, 72, 73, 75, 159–60, 182

Bards. *See* Religion, bardic

"Before I knocked," 91, 101, 102, 125, 175

Blake, William, 10, 25–27

passim, 33, 75, 76, 82, 93, 97, 105–06, 108–10, 113–15 *passim*, 119–20, 126–28, 133, 136, 142–43, 158, 159, 163, 164, 188

Bogs, 59, 66, 67, 68

Burke, Kenneth, 3, 17, 21, 24, 76

Burning Baby, The, 30–31

"Burning Baby, The," 30, 37–38, 50, 122, 123–24, 127, 162, 177

Campbell, Joseph, 8, 53, 53n, 56, 58, 65, 87

"Ceremony after a Fire Raid," 101, 182

Christianity. *See* Religion, Christian

Davies, Aneiran Talfan, 3–4, 8, 187

Davies, Edward, 6, 27, 59, 60, 61–62, 63, 65–66, 67, 69, 73, 75, 80–81, 86, 87, 90, 105, 113

Deaths and Entrances, 19

"Dress, The," 41, 140–41, 147, 161, 162, 176

Doom on the Sun, A, 112–13, 122, 127, 177. *See also* "Enemies, The"; "Holy Six, The"

"Do you not father me," 101, 133, 172

Dreams. *See* Unconscious, dreams

Druids, 55–58, 61, 65, 66, 86–88, 91, 92, 124. See also Mythology, Welsh

Early prose. See Prose, early

Egyptian mythology. See Mythology, Egyptian

Eighteen Poems, 19, 22, 63, 130

Emery, Clark, 184

"Enemies, The," 30, 37, 39–40, 41, 49, 50, 67, 97, 113–14, 138, 154, 159, 161, 176

"Especially when the October wind," 90

Evans, Caradoc, 11, 45–47

"Extraordinary Little Cough," 151, 181

"Fern Hill," 13, 182

"Fight, The," 13, 181

Fire. See Landscape imagery, sun and fire

FitzGibbon, Constantine, 4, 22, 189

Flood. See Landscape imagery, sea and flood

Frazer, Sir James, 53, 56, 80, 145

Freud, Sigmund, 18, 20, 24–25, 28, 71, 82, 83, 131, 133, 139, 141, 145, 147, 157, 193

"From love's first fever to her plague," 89

Frye, Northrop, 23, 28–29, 30, 104, 108, 127

Gardens and orchards. See Landscape imagery, gardens and orchards

"Gaspar, Melchior, Balthasar," 101–02, 121, 177

Graves, Robert, 6, 55, 57, 58, 61, 64, 72–73, 74, 79, 90, 134

"Grief thief of time," 22, 72, 116, 175

"Had she not loved me at the beginning," 145–46, 173

Hills, 66, 67, 69, 93, 96, 116

Hoffman, Frederick, 26, 28n

"Holy Six, The," 35, 36, 37, 39–40, 41, 46, 50, 67, 97, 107, 113, 114–16, 118, 119, 121, 123, 138, 154, 159, 161, 177

"Horse's Ha, The," 45, 49, 50, 97, 117, 122–23, 127, 178

"Hunchback in the Park, The," 158

"I dreamed my genesis," 99, 177

"I fellowed sleep," 125, 133, 176, 178

"If I were tickled by the rub of love," 101, 177

"I, in my intricate image," 67, 69, 92, 118–20, 178

"I make this in a warring absence," 116, 179

"Incarnate devil," 67, 175

"In country sleep," 10, 103, 163, 164, 165–67, 168, 182

Influences on Thomas' work: problems in source criticism, 6n, 22–29; of Christianity, 9; of early readings, 10–13; conscious and unconscious influences, 27–28; of Caradoc Evans, 45–47; of T. Y. Powys, 47–48; of Edward Davies, 59–60; of Welsh mythology,

60–63; of bardic religion, 86; of the occult, 108; of Blake, 127–28; of surrealism, 130–33, 135; "The Critics and the Problem of Influence," 184–90. *See also* Blake; Davies, Edward; Mythology; Occult; Religion; Surrealism

"In the beginning," 89, 176, 178

"In the Direction of the Beginning," 31, 36, 45, 72–74, 75, 78, 89, 95, 116, 117, 120, 149, 179

"In the white giant's thigh," 163, 183

"Into her Lying Down Head," 72, 111, 116, 165, 182

Islands. *See* Landscape imagery, islands

Ithel, Williams ab. *See* ab Ithel, Williams

Johnson, Pamela Hansford, 30, 42, 59, 64

Jones, Glyn, 8n, 99n, 124

Joyce, James, 47, 49, 54, 56, 152, 153, 191, 195, 196

Jung, C. G., 17–18, 21, 26, 28, 33, 52, 71, 193–94

"Just Like Little Dogs," 151, 152, 181

Kleinman, H. H., 186–88

Korg, Jacob, 20, 32, 41, 114, 115, 135, 187, 188

"Lament," 145, 183

Landscape imagery: around Swansea, 5; general treatment of, 13, 35–36, 40–41, 59–60,

62, 93–94, 96, 99, 114, 140; in "A Winter's Tale," 161–62

—bogs, 59, 66, 67, 68

—gardens and orchards, 59, 71, 75, 81, 82, 96–97, 99, 140, 143

—hills, 66, 67, 69, 93, 96, 116

—islands, 11, 35–36, 59–60, 66, 67, 72–74 *passim*, 75, 93, 116

—sea and flood, 35, 62–65, 66, 70–71, 75, 159, 160; in Thomas' poetry, 77–78

—sun and fire, 38, 62, 81, 83, 89–90, 93, 102–03, 123–24, 162

—valleys, 66, 92–93, 99–100, 113, 140

Langer, Suzanne, 37

Later prose. *See* Prose, later

Lawrence, D. H., 85, 149

"Lemon, The," 34, 41, 50, 117, 119, 120, 132–36, 138, 146–48 *passim*, 178

"Light breaks where no sun shines," 125, 176

Logos, 62, 73, 83, 84, 87, 89–90, 93, 96, 100, 104, 114, 131–32

Mabinogion, 64, 75, 87, 122

Machen, Arthur, 11–13, 56–57, 76, 79

Map of Love, The, 19, 20, 31, 72, 135, 160, 180, 181

"Map of Love, The," 35–37, *passim*, 47, 48, 50, 66–70, 71, 73, 74, 93, 94, 95, 97, 99, 107, 111, 116, 117, 124, 138, 141, 161, 178

"Martha," 15, 140, 141–42, 147, 176, 180

Maud, Ralph, 14, 19, 21, 23–25, 36, 85n, 173–83 passim

"Mouse and the Woman, The," 17, 18, 30, 37, 42, 78, 79, 81–82, 95, 111, 117, 132, 138, 142–46, 147, 162, 173, 178, 196

Moynihan, William T., 184

"Mr. Tritas on the Roofs." See "Orchards, The"

Murray, Margaret Alice, 6, 120, 125

"My hero bares his nerves," 125

Mysticism, 186–87, 188–89

Mythology: use of in Thomas' work, 13, 18, 27–28, 36–37, 50, 54, 59–60, 64–65, 76–77, 83–84, 116, 159, 168–69, 184–85; defined, 52

—Egyptian, 11, 37, 61–62, 70, 82, 84, 119, 126, 145

—Welsh, 5–6, 11, 37, 65–66, 72–73, 78–80 passim, 84, 122; history of, 55–63

"My world is pyramid," 68–69, 75, 77–78, 116, 159–60, 177

"No man believes," 125, 175

Notebook, Red. See Red Notebook

Notebooks, Poetry. See Poetry Notebooks

"Notes on the Art of Poetry," 131, 136, 147

"Not forever shall the lord of the red hail," 127, 175

"Not from this anger," 116, 174

Nowottny, Winifred, 25–27

Occult, 12, 19, 20, 50, 53–54, 79, 98, 104–05, 106, 107–08, 112; defined, 53–54. See also Logos

—witchcraft, 6, 15, 112, 115, 117, 120–21, 122–24

"Old Garbo," 152, 153, 180

Olson, Elder, 184–87

"One Warm Saturday," 153–54, 166, 180

Orchards. See Landscape imagery, gardens and orchards

"Orchards, The," 12, 30, 34, 41, 42, 50, 77, 78, 79–81, 90, 95–97, 98, 112, 114, 117, 124, 132, 136–38, 144, 147, 148, 156, 162, 177, 178

Organicism, 38, 50, 62, 87, 94, 105–07

"Over Sir John's hill," 163, 164, 182

Pantheism, 7, 85, 94–95

"Patricia, Edith, and Arnold," 13, 151, 152, 181

"Peaches, The," 13, 69, 151, 152, 179

"Poem on His Birthday," 75, 169, 182

Poetry Notebooks, 14–15, 19, 22, 72, 85, 89n, 121, 145–46; entries compared with prose for chronology, 173–83

Portrait of the Artist as a Young Dog, xi, 32, 33, 149, 152, 181

Powys, T. F., 11, 47

"Prologue to an Adventure," 48, 89–90, 155, 179

"Process in the weather of the heart, A" 77, 176

Prose: early, xi–xii, 31–23; comparison with later prose, xi–xii, 31–32, 149–51, 157, 168–69; style of, 12–13, 43–50; narrative method of, 13, 20–22, 28, 32, 33–37, 41, 49–50, 52, 83–84, 111, 128, 146–47; use of unconscious in, 34; use of metaphor in, 36–37, 40–42, 140, 146–47

—later, xi–xii, 31–33, 149–58; comparison with early prose, xi–xii, 31–32, 157, 168–69; style of, 149, 151

Prospect of the Sea, A, 32, 183
"Prospect of the Sea, A," 31, 35, 36, 40–41, 42–44 *passim*, 47, 50, 70–72, 74, 75, 81–82, 95, 96, 99, 110, 117, 124, 166, 178

"Quite Early One Morning," 158

Read, Sir Herbert, 128–29, 131, 147
Red Notebook, 14, 20, 20n, 30, 137, 138; dating of entries in, 173–78
"Refusal to Mourn, A," 102, 182
Religion: defined, 53, 85–104. *See also* Logos
—bardic, 53, 61, 86–98, 189–90
—Christian, 7–10, 38, 50, 61, 85–86, 87, 88, 91, 96, 98, 99, 100–03, 124, 125, 166
—mysticism, 186–87, 188–89
—pantheism, 7, 85, 94–95
—Unitarianism and the "New Learning," 7n, 8, 107
"Replies to an Enquiry," 18, 34n, 134n

"Saint about to fall, A," 75, 180
"School for Witches, The," 41, 50, 97, 112, 117, 120–21, 127, 159, 178
Sea and flood. *See* Landscape imagery, sea and flood
Selected Letters, 10, 17, 72
Sex, 14–15, 35–37, 38, 67, 69, 70, 75, 83, 84, 110, 114–15, 116, 124, 145, 164, 167
"Shiloh's seed," 107, 175
Snow, Lady Pamela. *See* Johnson, Pamela Hansford
Stanford, Derek, 16
Sun and fire. *See* Landscape imagery, sun and fire
Surrealism, 17–18, 20, 32, 48, 50, 134–35, 136–38, 139, 144, 147–48, 156. *See also transition*

"There was a Saviour," 25
Thomas, D. J. (Thomas' father), 8–9
Thomas, Dylan: biography, 1–22, 30–33, 59–60, 62–63, 125, 127–28; total work, 32–33, 157–58, 161, 164, 183
Thomas, Evan (Thomas' grandfather), 8
Thomas, William (Thomas' great-uncle), 8–9, 62, 107
"Three Poems," 164
Tindall, William York, 23, 35, 41, 48, 66, 85n, 107
"Today, this insect," 126, 128, 174, 179
transition, 16, 18, 52, 83, 132, 139n, 147; notes on contents of, 191–96. *See also* Surrealism

"Tree, The," 41–42, 44, 45, 98–101, 133, 137, 140, 161, 176
Treese, Henry, 17–18
Tritschler, Donald, 14, 20
"True Story." See "Martha"
Twenty-Five Poems, 19, 63, 130, 160

"Uncommon Genesis." See "Mouse and the Woman, The"
Unconscious, 21, 25–28 passim, 34, 50, 72, 77, 83, 107, 134, 148, 160, 168; distinguished from preconscious and Freudian unconscious, 28
—dreams, 12, 18, 24–26, 37, 39, 79, 80–82, 83, 95, 101, 129, 132–35, 136, 143–45, 147, 191, 195
Under Milk Wood, 32–33, 157–58, 161, 164, 183
Unitarianism, 7n, 8, 107
"Unluckily for a Death," 72, 116, 180

Valleys, 66, 92–93, 99–100, 113, 140
"Vest, The," 15, 140, 141, 147, 177
"Vision and Prayer," 10, 20, 102–03, 160–61, 165, 166, 182
"Visitor, The," 30, 34, 35, 44–45, 67, 90, 92–95, 98, 114, 118, 119, 132, 154, 159, 162, 177
"Visit to Granpa's, A," 13, 151, 180

Welsh mythology. See Mythology, Welsh
"When once the twilight locks no longer," 77, 160, 176
"Where once the water of your face," 116
"Where Tawe Flows," 152, 181
"Who Do You Wish Was With Us?" 151, 181
"Why east wind chills," 63, 175
Williams, Charles, 19, 104, 112, 117
"Winter's Tale, A," 20, 90, 161–63, 182
Witchcraft. See Occult, witchcraft
"Within his head revolved a little world," 139, 175
"World I Breathe, The." See "Map of Love, The"

Y Barddas. See ab Ithel, Williams; Religion, bardic